Caring for your Choir

CARING FOR YOUR CHOIR

A SEQUEL TO *I'M A CHOIR DIRECTOR??!*

POOGIE THE PUP
Publishing

DR. JOEL PLAAG

© 2023 Joel F. Plaag
All rights reserved.

First paperback edition: September 2023.

ISBN: 978-1-7373518-2-5
E-book ISBN: 978-1-7373518-3-2

Published by Poogie the Pup Publsihing
www.joelplaag.cc

Acknowledgements

First, to my editor-in-chief, Michelle, the librarian who stores a host of knowledge with her wherever she goes and spends time carefully making sure my sentences make sense.

For my wonderful assistant Debbie Rawlins, who continued to file music and keep everything organized while I ran off to write. She also got the first draft of this book and made sure the page numbers were right and got the contentious conversations on numbering or bullet points started.

To my favorite husband, Michael Rebner, who watched the dogs, took care of the house, and basically kept my home life together while I hunched over a computer, trying to pick active verbs instead of passive ones.

To my friends and family, who've always been the highlight of my existence.

Thanks to the many, many people who have either directly or indirectly helped me write this book. For those who commented and inspired me, and for those who continue to do so.

This continues to be a labor of love for the craft near and dear to my heart.

Table of Contents

PROLOGUE 1

PART ONE: PREPARATION 3
1. PREPARATION 4
    - WE GET TO KNOW OURSELVES 6
    - WE PREPARE MUSICALLY 6
    - WE FOCUS ON THE WORK 6
    - WE IMAGINE OUR IDEAL 7
    - WE EVALUATE 7
    - WHAT'S IN A LEADER? 7
    - FINDING OUR LEADER 8
    - ORGANIZATION 9
    - WHY ORGANIZE? 10
    - WHAT NOW? 10
2. A SPECIAL, SHARED TIME 11

- Leadership by importance 11
- About visibility 14
- What's our priority? 15
3. THE LIBRARY 16
- Folder numbers 17
- Copies 17
- Stuffing folders 18
- Collecting music 18
- The database 19
- The routine 20
4. CHALLENGE 21
5. CHOOSING MUSIC 26
- The choir diet 27
6. OWNERSHIP 29
- Volunteering 31
- Connecting with others 31
- A sense of purpose 31
- Closer to God 32
7. SPECIAL EVENTS 35
8. THE SPIRIT OF THE CHOIR 37
- The secret to the spirit of the choir 38
- Mission 38
- Aspirations 39
- Engaging others 40
- Spiritual growth 40
- About these areas 40
9. CONNECTING 43
- Special events – things to work for 43

RETREATS	44
TRIPS AND TOURS	45
HOSTING A GUEST CHOIR	45
FUNDRAISING	46
SINGING FOR AREA EVENTS	48
OTHER EVENTS	48
WRITING TO THE CHOIR	49

PART TWO: REHEARSALS 51
10. PACING REHEARSAL 52
INTRODUCTION	52
HARDEST PIECES FIRST	54
VARY THE REPERTOIRE	54
EASY MUSIC FIRST	55
SECTIONALS	55

11. REHEARSAL PATTERNS 57
PREPARING THE ORDER	57
TEN-TO-FIFTEEN MINUTES	57
DIVIDE AND CONQUER	58
MANAGE THE BITES	58
CLOCK RULES	58
VARYING THE ACTIVITIES	59

12. THE REHEARSAL PLAN 60
PHYSICAL	60
BREATH	61
VOCAL	61
THIS SUNDAY	63
ALTERNATE FIRST PIECE – THE HARDEST	63

    Announcements 64
    Ending the Rehearsal 64
13. MANAGING REHEARSAL 66
    Introducing a piece of music 66
    The only part that matters 67
    Here's a taste 68
    Teaching the notes 68
    Sectionals... 69
    Two-by-two... 69
    Dictated notes 70
    If all else fails….. 70
    Back in context.. 71
    Ignoring as reward 71
    Keeping it real 71
    Closing a section 73
    Mini performance... 74
    Parts to whole 74
    An unsuccessful ending..................................... 75
14. FINAL REHEARSAL 76
    The logistical rehearsals 76
    Seating... 77
    Final run-throughs... 78
    The punch list 79
    The last choir rehearsals 80
    Preparing for the orchestra 81
    Final thoughts 82
15. COMMUNICATING 83
    Why should we stop?.. 84

- Continual errors 84
- Catastrophic failure 85
- Reinforcing 85
- Pushing through the problems 86
- Final thoughts on when to stop 86

PART THREE: CONCERTS 87
16. JUST BEFORE THE CONCERT 88
- The piano rehearsal 89
- The orchestral rehearsal 90
- Breaks 91
- Marking the music 92
- The orchestral rehearsal order 93
- Keeping everyone together 93
- Adding winds and brass 93
- The voice versus orchestra 94

17. CONCERT DAY 96
- Starting the Day Right 97
- Final pre-concert reminders 98
- A sense of rhythm 98

18. LASTING MOMENTS 100
- Acknowledging applause 101
- Before the music 101
- After each piece 101
- Starting a new piece 102
- The end 103

19. ERRORS 105
- Identifying the problem 107

COMMUNICATING THE SOLUTION 108
20. AFTER THE CONCERT 110
    THE RECEPTION 112
    STAYING CONNECTED AFTER 112

PART FOUR: THE INTERNAL WORK 115
21. THE WHOLE SINGER 116
    LIFE CYCLE EVENTS 116
    JOYS AND CONCERNS 117
    BRINGING IN NEWCOMERS 118
22. LISTENING 120
23. REJECTION 124
    TAKING INVENTORY 126
    DEALING WITH REJECTION 130
    BETRAYAL 131
    DON'T TAKE IT PERSONALLY 132
24. SELF-CARE 133
    GUIDES FOR SELF-CARE 135
    PRACTICE GRATITUDE 136
    TAKING BREAKS 136
    PRIORITIZE 137
    CHANGE THE PERSPECTIVE 137
    PRAY 137
    OUR TIME 138
    NOBODY'S PERFECT 138
25. RECONNECTION 141
    THE BREATH 142
    THE CONNECTION 143

    FINDING BOTH BREATH AND CONNECTION 144
    CAN GOD BE IN THERE, TOO? 147
EPILOGUE..150
    PREPARING FOR THE NEXT HURDLE 151
ABOUT THE AUTHOR..153

Prologue

The yellow notepad sits in the next room with CHRISTMAS CONCERT scrawled at the top in the most menacing way. It's the middle of July, and I don't want to look at it yet. I don't want to decide what instruments to use. I don't want to make sure that I have enough scores, enough instrumental parts, and enough money to start this new project we affectionately call "Christmas." Though everything is slow right now, I know we will start rehearsals soon, and the path to December 25 is short.

That will wait.

Right now, it's time to take care of the most important part of my choir – me. This means not answering the phone for a few minutes. It means taking that trip across the state to visit a friend. It means slowing down, pacing myself, and enjoying the day-to-day monotony of the heat, the planning, and the preparing for August's untimely arrival.

"It'll still be there tomorrow," my dad used to say to his coworkers as they hurried through the afternoons into early evenings, coding long strings of programs together in off-white cubicles. The same applies to choir directors; we prepare, we plan, and we make beautiful things happen, but it doesn't all have to be right now.

For right now, come with me as we explore some of the practical tips of rehearsing the church choir.

If you're reading this, you've already got a sense of curiosity, a love of music, and a feeling that between you and those volunteers, anything is possible. You try to make a difference in other people's lives. You work hard preparing for rehearsals and performances. You enjoy a great love of music – the performing, the phrases, and the way it all fits together makes sense to you.

Additionally, you face challenges making sure rehearsals are interesting. You want the group to leave feeling energized. You love rehearsing, but sometimes don't know if the extra things like concert preparations, day-to-day tasks, or final rehearsals are going the way you want them to go.

This book is for you.

PART ONE: PREPARATION

1.
PREPARATION

One hour to go. *Tick-tock.*

Just weeks earlier, I was driving through New Mexico on a badly needed, week-long vacation. Stopping overnight in the town of Jemez Springs as part of my solo sojourn, I wandered into the Highway 4 Café.

Filled with mini quiches, donuts and quickly made omelets, the Highway 4 Café was the only place for breakfast within 30 miles. I found a small table inside as people milled around in the cool mountain air. It was early Monday morning, and no one was thinking about choir rehearsals.

I needed inspiration. I had been working seven days a week, meeting with contractors, learning new lights and sound systems, and preparing for the opening of the performance hall. Final checklists were ready, and I had to

Preparation

pull over after several phone calls to walk workers through powering up the different stage systems that I had only been trained on a few days before.

Here in this remote village in the Jemez Mountains, I was more interested in reading my novel, so I didn't really notice when a woman sat down at the table across from me. Like me, she was alone, and after ordering her food, asked me if I was enjoying my book.

Though I really wasn't interested in conversation, she excitedly discussed her latest read. She told me she was a poet. She described how she had started writing to help others. When she found out I had already authored a book, she analyzed me quickly.

"What made you decide to write about choir directing?"

I hadn't really thought about it. I felt a compulsion after finishing a conducting workshop. I had some great tricks that I learned, and I wanted others not to suffer like I did when I was learning to direct.

When I told her what this book was about, she again commented, "You like to help people."

I explained my philosophy on choral music. I love talking about this and became very giddy as my response bubbled out in a flood of words.

Choral music is something we do together. We use our bodies to create something that none of us could do alone. It's a connection with one another in a very intimate, very real way. In fact, when singing in a choir, none of us exist as single individuals anymore. We act as a group – faithfully leading and following one another.

"Choral music is a way to help people," I agreed. "It's also a way to *heal* people."

We come to rehearsal in various states of disarray. Our families may not like us today. Our spouses may be upset. We may have had a dreadful day at work or wrecked the car. But each of us comes to rehearsal and we begin. We start the work reconnecting with one another by singing. It doesn't matter our political affiliations, our theological views, our relationship status, or even our state of mind. Once we sing the first note, it all goes by the wayside.

I help people forget themselves for a few minutes or for an hour or two.

By forgetting ourselves, we become closer to God.

It starts with getting our minds right as directors. How do we carry out this seemingly impossible task?

We get to know ourselves

We ask ourselves: what are my strengths and weaknesses as a musician? Do I sing well? Do I play the piano? Do I have a philosophy of why choral music is so important? Do I acknowledge my limitations?

We prepare musically

Next we examine: have I learned the piece and how to direct it? Can I sing each line alone *a cappella?* Do I know where the entrances are and how to help others find them?

We focus on the work

The director *directs.* We aren't here for explanations or philosophy. We just direct. We practice gestures with a mirror. Does it look convincing and clear? Practice singing parts aloud while sitting at the piano. Imagine cuing the choir at various places while playing. We ask: can I look in the right direction for the cues? Does my gesture embody the music at hand?

We imagine our ideal

Am I funny and silly? Tough? Pushing? Encouraging? We must envision our leadership style before setting foot in front of the choir. Are we worried about the notes and phrasing? Is our main goal to have the choir enjoy their time together? Is our goal to create a professional ensemble? Do we believe in what we're doing?

We evaluate

Were we successful in today's rehearsal? Was it fun? Did we take too long on any one part? Did we treat everyone well? Was it an effort? Were we afraid? Did we feel like we knew what we were doing? Did we know the music well enough to teach it? If not, how can we improve? Was the problem in our heads? Did we seem impatient or understanding toward others? Did we act like a big shot or respond with humility?

What's in a leader?

Each of us leads differently, so it's important to find our authentic leadership style. At first, many of us want to emulate some of our mentors such as former professors or conducting teachers. While this is okay in starting the process, it can hamper us from becoming at ease with ourselves in the rehearsal room.

Finding our leader

On a piece of paper, write some good and bad attributes of being a choir director. Is your ideal director funny? Cerebral? How does that person talk to the choir? How does this person get their ideas of sound across? It could look like this:

A good director:	*A bad director:*
Embodies.	Explains.
Learns.	Tells.
Reacts.	Demands.
Suggests.	Orders.
Empowers.	Tells.
Inspires.	Defines.
Empathizes.	Makes.
Focuses.	Distracts.

Describe your favorite choir rehearsal. Was it funny? Serious? Were choristers pointed out who did things well? What specifically caused you to choose that rehearsal over the others?

Return to the list above showing the director's good and bad traits. Does your list look like that list? Which traits do you have? (You can be honest here; this list is between you and me, not your choir.) How can you replace bad traits with good ones?

Preparation

Two days ago, I sent out the rehearsal order. Certain people will email if I didn't get the notes out, or if I didn't present a story or two. Once that email is out, I know where I'm headed in rehearsal because the organization work is done.

Organization

Speaking of organization, in what order are we rehearsing each piece? How long does each piece last? Can this week's problems be fixed in ten minutes? If not, how small of a section can be used to create a ten- or fifteen-minute success? Is it urgent that we get it perfect today?

In graduate school, my wonderful choir *endured* rehearsals because I couldn't organize my time. Since they were young adults, they grew restless. I dreaded rehearsals more and more because I felt so much shame and guilt that they weren't efficient or fun. After one particularly bad rehearsal I went to my professor, embarrassed because I didn't know what to do.

"Have you tried creating a minute-by-minute rehearsal plan, like I do?" he asked, and with a lot more patience than I would have asked.

Embarrassed, I said, "No."

I promised him I would try it and left his office. I wrote plans, breaking down rehearsal into ten-minute increments. To this day, I am grateful that the man did not shame me for ignoring his teaching. Instead, he waited until I gave up my own idea and asked him for help.

I still create a minute-by-minute plan, and allow the clock, rather than the outcome, to dictate how long to rehearse each piece.

Why organize?

People prefer to come to rehearsal if they know what's going to happen. They want a certain amount of routine. Although no two rehearsals are alike, people want to have some anticipation when they come so they know what is expected. Besides, it makes it easier on us.

Something unique to the church choir is that the repertoire is always changing and may be recycled every few months. In school choirs, we learn a few pieces, prepare them for a single concert, perform, and put them away for years. In church choir, we perform the same pieces sporadically with the same people. Since the same people perform the music, the amount of rehearsal time can be far less.

What now?

You've found yourself in front of a volunteer choir. Congratulations! Many of my friends have found themselves in front of church choirs by accident. Follow the process. Find confidence in your own ability. Stay organized. Communicate your expectations. And if all else fails, ask for help. Though real humility means saying, "I don't know," it also means, "I can do this."

2.
A Special, Shared Time

Caring for the choir isn't easy. In fact, it's probably one of the hardest things we do as choir directors. We accommodate, we cajole, we pray for, we support, and we show an air of confidence and ability toward our singers.

It may not always be enough.

It's never a worthless venture, though. We stretch. We demonstrate. And we learn.

Leadership by importance

Leadership by importance creates a sense of urgency when describing the time in rehearsal. It communicates our expectations upfront, so that the choir knows what to expect from us.

The leader must come ready to address, at a moment's notice, the importance of today's rehearsal. We must demonstrate that importance with urgency, directness, some levity, and an absolute focus on the resulting performance.

The music we create is essential to build that importance, and we can do that by picking music we genuinely like and by rehearsing it all the way through. In fact, it's why we're in rehearsal – to prepare the music.

The second reason of emphasizing importance is the connection singers have with one another. We do this work because we can't do it alone, and regularly we communicate that to our singers by thanking them for a great rehearsal, starting on time and spending most of the time singing.

The third reason for emphasizing importance is the connection with one another. Each of our choristers can find places to sing, but knowing each person's ensemble strengths and challenges as a gives our singers a sense of belonging.

A long time ago, a wonderful professor came to conduct a junior college festival choir in my state. Well-gifted as a conductor and with great music at the ready, she was already prepared for a successful weekend of singing with the mostly young adult crowd.

It was the first communication with the choir in the opening minutes that amazed me. With a soft voice, she stood up on the podium, having never seen these people before. She smiled and raised her hand, waiting until there was silence. Next, without any fanfare, admonishing or browbeating, she quietly told the choir what she expected.

A Special, Shared Time

"We have such a *special, shared time* together, and it's so limited," (emphasizing importance) "and since it is so limited, I would hope that you would bring your water to your chair, and only use the restroom if absolutely necessary," (creating an expectation.) Then she continued.

"I know you're as excited as I am about doing this concert, so can we try to stay focused during our rehearsals and make our time together really special?"

This was a masterclass in ensemble expectation and classroom control. Those students went wild during the breaks, but when the choir rehearsal was going on, no sound was made, and the focus was absolute.

It didn't hurt matters that during the many hours of rehearsal the conductor had them marching around the room to work on beat precision, use their hands to develop the contours of phrases, and sit in diverse groups, creating variety.

But it all started with a simple expectation – that the choir members would stay focused and out of the restroom.

This sense of importance expands into other areas as well. We prepare concerts for audiences off campus and around the world. We clean and move instruments. We organize the choir room and the library. We host fundraising events – dinners and markets and auctions and choir festivals – and more.

It's a lot of work, but there's a serious reason. If we want to have an orchestra every spring and Christmas, we must do the work to prepare. The same is true for our fundraisers throughout the year. There's a sense of intention and earnestness in preparing for these events. They're important to everyone, and there is a recognizable goal.

Concerts require the same urgency. We work hard to prepare for them and in so doing we make a difference in others' lives. Our Sunday morning fare, which could easily be relegated to the back burner, becomes essential because we know how much it means to the people in the audience, including former singers who may not be able to participate anymore.

Our concerts are part of a larger ritual connecting to the season. We sing a concert, and our audience says, "now Christmas can begin!" They listened to our spring concert, and they say how much they enjoyed it; how they didn't know the piece before.

Through our sense of importance, we telegraph that essentiality to others, making them feel that what we do is important. In the life of church – or in school, college, or university, if we treat choir as an essential part of what we do, then it telegraphs to others.

About visibility

Despite our best efforts, sometimes we have a low turnout. Our concerts may result in an audience of only a small handful. Once my college choir sang at a church where the choir outnumbered the audience almost two to one.

We did it anyway.

We can't be distracted by an imaginary attendance check at the room. We have better things to do than ask,

A Special, Shared Time

"Who was missing from the audience? Who bothered to come?"

It's a destructive behavior that while seeming normal and acceptable, really is dangerous and damaging both to you and the choir. What if no one comes to our concerts? Is it really a testament to your ability as director? And what message does your defeatism send to the ensemble?

We never wonder why the audience isn't there. It's damaging both for us and our choir.

What's our priority?

It takes a lot. Yes, it feels all-consuming. Yes, it may seem like there's never any time away for our own pursuits. But at the end of the day, when we stand up in front of the group and get to make *music*, the reward speaks for itself. We get to perform. We care for our ensemble because they come week after week, and often they care for us, too.

3.
THE LIBRARY

Choirs love a sense of ownership over their "stuff." They write notes, draw, maybe annotate how to find entrances, mark breaths, and generally feel a sense of belonging to their beloved octavos.

It makes sense that people develop an attachment to their music. They might take it home to play it or listen to recordings to get the notes right.

One day the unthinkable happens – we finish using the music, take it away, and stick it in a file cabinet. Months or years later we pull it back out and hope they remember it. Each person tries to claim his old score, but not everyone succeeds. Some choristers take new music with the wrong part highlighted. Next, the re-teaching begins, since not everybody has all the old markings.

One choir member used to *notoriously* collect so many new copies of music we called this compulsion the "Buddy" award. When the music ran out, I looked through his folder. Buddy often had three or four copies of the current anthem. Each week Buddy saw the piles of music on the table and picked up new copies of the same pieces! Occasionally other choir members would do the same thing, unaware that their folder contained all the music for rehearsal. As additional members hoarded their own sets of music, we bestowed the Buddy Award on them. Though Buddy has since passed away, his award lives on.

What's not cute is when newcomers didn't have all their music because so many copies had been hoarded by Buddy and his acolytes! Now we have a system.

Folder numbers

Most choirs have folders and are assigned folder numbers so they can find their own music. If yours doesn't, or if you just put music on their chairs before rehearsal, give each person a space – a cubby hole, organizing box, dividers; whatever you wish – so that it's *their* spot.

Copies

If we place music on the table for anyone to pick up at the beginning of rehearsal, the choir will constantly search the pile for "their" copy. Wouldn't it be better if "their" copy was always in "their" folder? A straightforward way to do this is to number each copy of music so it matches the folder numbers. Then, when it's time to pass out a new piece, it takes about two minutes more to insert everyone's music into their folder slots. This means each time we prepare the music, it already has their markings on it.

Stuffing folders

Many of us have plenty of other things to do, including preparing for the next rehearsal. We can ask people in the choir to pull music and place it in folders. On Wednesday nights, all choir members pass in their music so it can be brought to the sanctuary. After church on Sunday morning, the music is collected. One choir member, when she sees a newcomer, grabs a folder, and assigns that folder to them. This frees me to practice for rehearsal.

Collecting music

For years, I had a "method." I kept boxes near the exits for music so as the choir finished concerts, choristers could leave the music in the box.

Some people forgot. Others didn't go near the box. Some saw the box and forgot to drop off their music. Ultimately, I had to track singers down – going on a paper-laden safari. I'd remind them before the next rehearsal. I'd offer to meet them at the church; at their house; at the car wash, wherever they wanted!

How can we possibly get all this music picked up after it's been performed? How can we get all those weekly works collected without having to search out our singers? It's an unending task.

Magically, the choir developed a culture of turning in their own music. They started passing it in during rehearsal and several turned it in to our librarian. Suddenly, collecting and storing music became stress-free! Some still take their music home, and our librarian still ventures after them, but the number of people she must find has gone down dramatically!

The database

None of us became choir directors to spend hours in front of the computer, but it's sometimes necessary. At a former church, the music was in drawers in dusty filing cabinets. The inventory sat in a little box of index cards, marked with the dates the anthems had been used. Eventually, we learn to make a database. Today we use Excel, but there are many other programs to make the inventory searchable.

Assign a number to each piece. We have an alphabetical-number system, so A's are 100's, B's are 200's, and they go from there, so that when a file comes between #175, *Ave Maria* and #180, *Ave Verum Corpus,* we can add a number in between like #178, *Ave Maris Stella.* Other libraries I've seen use numbers in order of date purchased; the higher numbers mean the newer pieces. Most importantly the title, the composer, the publisher, and date published are listed in the database. Today, when we must note the publishing information for livestream, it's much easier to have it handy in the database rather than looking it up in the score.

Databases can show if there are solos, how difficult the piece is, when it was last performed, and if there is instrumental accompaniment. In my hand bell choir, seeing the difficulty rating allows me to judge in a few seconds if a new song would be right for the group.

The routine

Even for a free-spirited choir director, a well-organized library helps to focus on the job at hand and out of the library. With a little work, any choir will enjoy a good working routine where everyone gets their same music, everyone knows where the music is, and everyone has a hand in keeping the music organized.

4.
CHALLENGE

What have I done to myself??

Pushing chairs across the stage, I wondered why, on a Sunday afternoon, I was sitting on the stage alone, sweating profusely while setting up risers – huge ones; the heavy, smooth wooden ones with the metal legs. It was a new hall with new items. It was a hall built for theater, and the acoustics were not great. That final two weeks of rehearsals pushed me hard, and though I had experience directing, I had never done anything quite like this. It was the first performance of my newly formed community chorus singing Haydn's *Lord Nelson Mass*, sung by a choir made of people from all over central Texas.

As I started this project, I was introduced to Linda, a wonderful, energetic church musician. Linda lived and worked in my new hometown for many years and knew a lot of the community singers. She was a professional organist who was driven, brilliant, and excited to work on this project.

Together we planned and plotted: letters to all the area choral directors, emails and letters to the defunct choral society singers, and phone calls to various people around town. We even reached out to communities more than fifty miles away. We had one goal: to start this choir with a bang.

Linda arranged for rehearsal space at the local Catholic church while I sat up in my office, day after day, contacting the big and small churches. I met with pastors, choir directors, community singers, and leaders from the town. I held my breath to see the result. At the end of the summer, I had a choir of over thirty and those thirty joined another forty students from the local college, creating a massed group.

My fascination with the Haydn *Lord Nelson Mass* started as an undergraduate when I first heard the delicious soprano solo in the *Kyrie*. The austerity and fear of the opening movement was exciting. But I had never performed the work all the way through.

Why not try? What did I have to lose?

I called for a three-hour rehearsal on Monday nights. One of my new section leaders refused to rehearse that long. Another potential member was sure it would never work. My colleagues made sure to tell me I had lost my mind. As a newcomer in town at my first full-time college teaching job, I lacked any history or experience to tell me it was supposed to fail.

Challenge

I was desperate. I needed two more conducting recitals to finish my degree. I couldn't let a little thing like reality stop me from preparing this concert. We met in a dimly lit, beautiful Catholic church, and I was genuinely surprised. I begged and pleaded with diverse groups – the Hotel Occupancy Tax board, my school, various community members, and somehow came up with the money to hire a professional orchestra from Houston.

Rehearsals began and so did the best part: "snack time." Each week various choir members tried to outdo one another with their baked goods. I taught parts in little classrooms and conducted with Linda at the piano in the sanctuary. We sat in circles late into the evening, learning notes, striving, and working. As the weeks progressed, a growing excitement began to spread through the choir.

The numbers grew. People came, week after week, to rehearse. As one week led to the next, my first community chorus began to take shape before my eyes. But it was more than that; I watched the members bubbling with excitement about the challenging work they were doing. Every week they came with their scores, practiced in between rehearsals, and seemed genuinely excited about the upcoming concert.

Finally, the dress rehearsal came. This small town had a big choir of more than seventy people. They came from everywhere; from other towns and far-flung rural counties, commuting long distances in the dark. But they came, wide-eyed and excited. The orchestra played beautifully, despite my racing pulse. With my ever-present nerves in tow, we sailed through our first concert.

"What are we going to do next?" they asked, and the eager choir was born.

In those days, I was dumb enough to not think, *we can't do that.* It started with trying something that hadn't been done before. Create a choir in a small town by running around and begging churches to send me their singers, fundraise, hire an orchestra, and perform the *Lord Nelson Mass.* What could possibly go wrong?

That day on the stage, as I sat putting the risers up by myself, I decided I was in over my head. I shouldn't be doing this; I had come too far, too fast. At that point, I was already into it. The contract was signed, the hall rented, and the orchestra engaged.

Up until that afternoon dragging out those chairs, it was all just rehearsal, and none of that really mattered. But now it was *real.* I had neglected the part where I rationally thought about doing an orchestra concert. I didn't stop and think about the outcomes or what an experienced choir director would do.

In other words, I was dumb enough to just jump in and try to figure out the details later.

The choir was so excited, and it kept me going. They loved the piece and really wanted to perform it, so in the moments where I sat and wondered what I was thinking, it was too late. Those weeks of phone calls, emails, letters, and meetings had paid off. Now the choir was supporting me.

Challenge

We never did earn back all the money we spent on that concert, but it propelled us forward into a new era of music making. We gained new members and within two years would travel to New York as the little choir from the small town.

It's good to "play it safe" when programming. One could even say it's logical to not push the choir beyond their presumed ability. We could have sung some pieces with piano or something much easier, but sometimes it's worth taking a risk. Take a trip. Hire that orchestra. Perform that giant "mountain top" work. It's worth it.

For a choir, doing the same music over and over gets old. Singing music that doesn't challenge creates a sense of antipathy. They'll come because they like you, but the challenge – whether it be taking a trip, stretching the abilities with instrumentalists, performing a tough piece, or preparing for a prestigious locale, choirs love to do things that put them over the top, and, in turn, bring in more choir members.

Sometimes we must be just silly enough to try, even when we may fail.

5.
Choosing Music

The rehearsal process starts the minute the previous rehearsal ends. There's a momentary sigh of relief that the last rehearsal plan worked. After that, when the last person leaves and we can sit, we have a moment to process the rehearsal. What just happened? Did I like it?

There are three reasons people keep coming back. First, the music is worth their time. Second, they feel a sense of responsibility to the other members of the choir – and *maybe* you (but not as much.) Third, they feel like the choir is a respite from the rest of the week.

Selecting repertoire, our first criteria, is one of the most critical things we can do by ourselves. We'll talk about the feeling of responsibility and their desire for respite in the next chapter.

Choosing Music

The choir diet

What does your choir diet look like? Is it all "old favorites?" Are there challenging pieces? Do you program mostly hymn arrangements? Are there other languages?

New directors should take some time to research. What music has the choir performed in the last five years? If there's not a list, there may be old bulletins or emails, or ask the choir what music they recently performed. This might procure a list of "favorite" anthems, but it's not really going to give an exhaustive list for the purposes of learning the choir's ability.

After directing the choir for several years, it's obvious already which pieces they like, which pieces present challenges, and where their reading ability is. Find new pieces – or pieces new to the choir. Look for older music; pieces never performed, or music we own has never been performed. Look critically, asking several questions.

- What is the text? Can we use it for general year-round church services? Is it just for Advent or Christmas? Does the text match the message on Sunday mornings? If not, is there some historical or cultural reason to choose this piece? Though music and accessibility are the paramount part of selecting a piece of music, the text is just as important.
- Is the music interesting? Is there counterpoint? Does the meter change or do the harmonies go in unexpected directions? Is there some technique that can be taught? Are they ready?

Caring for Your Choir

- Is there enough time to teach the piece? It may mean splitting into sectional rehearsals with volunteers leading. It also may mean using extra time in each rehearsal for a few months to teach the score.
- Is it memorable? Does the piece make you want to keep singing it? Will the choir leave rehearsal humming or will they begrudgingly struggle to learn the music? If the choir doesn't love the music at first – especially if it's hard – that doesn't mean it should be thrown away. If *you* are convinced it is exciting, and *you* are ready to tackle the work, then it's memorable. Though not every choir member will like every piece, if they groan after several weeks of rehearsing it, a new piece might be needed.
- Do you love the music?

With a choir that's supportive – most directors have supportive choirs – and you love the music, the choir will most likely come around. They eventually will learn to love the piece too.

6.
Ownership

Escorting guest choirs, cooking meals, hosting outside events, creating dinner theater programs – all these and more create ownership in the choir program. Our goal is to continue to make money so we can support hiring an orchestra for two concerts a year. To make that happen, we host many events. Our people volunteer to do these because they directly contribute to the upcoming concerts. They operate the sound system, run stage lights, clean, move equipment, and run choral festivals. In short, the choir does work outside of rehearsal to prepare for time in rehearsal.

The highlight of our fundraising is still the annual craft show. One person runs point, working with vendors through the entire year and developing relationships with them. We set up the spaces, organize the vendors, direct the throngs of people who pass through the doors, provide entertainment, bake snacks for sale, organize health department and fire department permits, pass out programs, host elementary school choirs, provide hospitality carts to the vendors, and clean the spaces after each day, often restocking the restrooms and taking out trash. Within hours of its close, we return the entire church back to normal.

We do all this work for one goal – to prepare for the Christmas and Spring concerts. These events do more than raise money. They give the choir a sense of ownership in financial affairs. By doing these fundraisers, they feel connected and willing to give more of their time.

Each one of these fundraising events needs workers, but they're a lot of fun and help us bond. We get to spend a little time together learning about one another. We get to see one member's quilting project; we hear about another member's family; we grieve with another's struggles at work.

All these touching moments come in the brief pauses between choirs at the festivals, or as the sandwiches are being wrapped, or as the hallways are swept. We bond to one another in the down-time moments when we're moving toward our common goal of raising money for our choir.

Ownership means that we don't have to guilt our members to sing for us; they always come. It means that there's space for them in our choir whether they are professional musicians, expert sandwich-makers, or good crowd-controllers. It just means everyone has a place for their unique gifts.

Ownership

Volunteering

Why do people volunteer? What brings people in? Why do they continue giving their time?

Connecting with others

Every year at a national church music conference during the summer we perform as a massed choir for daily chapel services and a concert at the end of the week. As part of this massed choir, I sit next to strangers, and I think I will never be able to connect with them. They all seem to know one another, and I'm immediately an outsider. However, after a few minutes singing with these other volunteers, we have something to talk about – music! By lunch that first day, I got to know many of them – people who I wouldn't have otherwise met.

Because I was involved in an activity, the usual barriers were broken. Instead, we enjoyed a common shared experience. This experience enabled me to connect with my new acquaintances.

Volunteering gives us a means to create those connections by bypassing awkward, unstructured initial interrogations. We immediately have something to talk about.

A sense of purpose

"I take care of my wife," he said. "It's the only time I get out of the house."

"With my husband gone, I look forward to doing something with others."

"It allows me to forget my job for a while."

I have heard these, and more reasons people come to rehearsals. Some people's reasons break my heart. They join the choir because they're lonely. They join because they're in need of something besides their job. Others just need to sing as a distraction.

In this way, volunteering – and singing – gives people a sense of purpose. We as directors must make it worth their while. We can create good, flowing rehearsals. We can organize social events. We can help engage members who need a little extra care by giving them a safe space.

We can't be every member's therapist, counselor, or sounding board, but we can cultivate a community so that they can be one another's help. We can organize potluck events, Christmas parties and pool parties, and create reasons for people to come together.

Closer to God

Approaching the center of the labyrinth and still contemplating the question *why we volunteer*, I encountered a rock in the center. *God*, the voice whispered.

Some of us are religious; some spiritual; others agnostic, but no volunteer is exempt from the experience of the otherness of God (or The Universe, The Great Spirit, whatever you wish to call it.) Choir is just a means to experience the divine collectively. Volunteer choirs allow us to feel that connection when we reach those magical high points. Our job, as directors, is to get to those points as efficiently as possible. We might look at the history that inspired someone to write a piece of music, or examine their unique patterns of writing, but ultimately staying in the moment is where that experience happens.

I remember conducting the orchestra in Romania one afternoon. It was one of my favorite sections in the third movement of Shostakovich's *Symphony No. 5*. After a slow, emotive climb, the emotional climax comes at the end, when the strings, now playing softly, become background to the light touch of the celeste touching the central theme for the last time. Alone, listening to a recording, this would be a knockout, but surrounded by the focused players, conducting this piece in a hot, un-air-conditioned hall, I held my breath, conducting as little as possible. As we reached that magical moment, I heard a siren wailing away through the open hall doors. The chaos erupting just outside juxtaposed with the absolute stillness of the celeste playing Shostakovich's haunting melody shut me down. I was an extra in this scene, relegated to the status of a prop or light fixture. I didn't matter here; I just existed.

I never wanted that moment to end.

That's where God exists; in those sublime moments where we are swept away by a world that moves forward despite our actions. Volunteering – especially in music – regularly hands us those still, quiet spaces. When volunteering helps us make music, we experience those moments in a personal way.

This is the most important thing we can give to our choirs; and why, ultimately, they keep coming back. We hand them a sense of otherworldliness that is shared and yet deeply personal all at the same time. In short, we help them experience the divine.

7.
Special Events

It's time to build two table-top fountains.

Fountains have nothing to do with choir directing, running community choruses, or preparing choirs for a concert, except today they do. At the end of August, we'll host one of our major fundraisers – the dinner and Broadway show. Since part of the show is a silent auction, we'll give away some electronics, some sports memorabilia, some general "stuff," and some delightful homemade crafts, including my fountains. Meanwhile, many choir members will prepare food, including crock pots full of pastas, bowls of salads and the obligatory garlic bread.

These special events give us something to look forward to, and present. But they also work their way into our mission – bringing choral music to Northwest Houston, and our desire to connect with others through our concerts.

Caring for Your Choir

Once while teaching, my college choir was preparing for a trip to New York. Though they had regular, manageable payments, they needed some extra ways to pay for their trips. So we sold pies, arranging delivery at Thanksgiving from a famous pie company in Houston. The students earnestly worked, getting orders and money so they could buy the pies. The day before the break, I drove into the city with another teacher, loaded my old Explorer full of pies, and passed them out to the students to deliver. The students earned money and felt engaged that they had worked hard to prepare for their trip.

Special events provide us with tasks that can be done by everyone. Some last-minute details have nothing to do with music. Before contests, we've fixed light ballasts and swept floors. We've moved the folders and furniture. We tucked hand bells and tables into closets. We also cleared out classrooms. We blocked off driveways with flags and barrels, preparing for the onslaught of visitors. Choir members came and spent all day running bookstores and snack bars. We've even hung banners for our concert, passed out advertising postcards, knowing that our next concerts are just a few weeks away.

Our special events remind us of the effort involved in performing our concerts. They allow us to work with one another outside of rehearsal, connecting us together with additional friends and family. Most importantly, our special events reinforce that our mission of bringing good choral music encompasses more than just day-to-day rehearsals.

8.
THE SPIRIT OF THE CHOIR

The Spirit of the Lord is upon me
Because He hath anointed me to preach the
gospel to the poor
To preach deliverance to the captive
And recovery of sight to the blind
To preach the acceptable year of the Lord.
To give unto them that mourn a garland for
ashes
The oil of joy for morning,
A garland of praise for the spirit of heaviness
That they might be called trees of righteousness.

Like it or not, the spirit of the choir is upon us. Choir members reflect the feeling we give. If we're super-critical, our choirs will be too. If we're standoffish, our choirs will also be standoffish.

Caring for Your Choir

And if we act like they're not important, they'll get the message.

What makes up the "spirit" of the choir? Is it having a good time working toward a common goal? Is it having a moderately difficult task and slowly, week after week, addressing and overcoming that task? Is it constant reliance on God?

Yes, it's all this, and more.

The spirit of the choir is the feeling that exists in the members of the group. It inspires enthusiasm, devotion, and a strong regard for the honor of the group. It occurs when the choir has positive experiences that are hard-won, such as a concert well done, a trip completed or a group project well- received.

The secret to the spirit of the choir

Building a spirit of togetherness starts with having a clear and unambiguous mission. Do we want to sing with orchestras? Travel? Prepare new or more challenging works? Does our group meet on Sunday mornings and wish to reach more people through music? What about healing? What about the release from daily drudgery?

This exercise is one to help focus five aspects of choir membership: mission, aspirations, engaging others, and spiritual growth.

Mission

What is the choir known for?

- Difficult repertoire

The Spirit of the Choir

- Travel
- Fundraising
- Hosting other choirs (college choirs, youth choirs)
- A big voice in the church governance
- Annual concerts
- Weekly/monthly events (prayer services, workshops, lectures, concerts)
- Great leadership (Sunday school, bible studies, etc.)
- Creating a special musical event
- Children's or youth choir support
- Good hymn arrangements
- Great food/meals
- Parties
- Premiering new compositions

Aspirations

If money wasn't a hindrance, what are some goals for the choir?

- Travel more
- Perform more concerts
- Host workshops for other choirs
- Have more celebrations, including parties and potlucks
- Create multiple ensembles
- Create a sound and light ministry
- Add high school or college choristers

Caring for Your Choir

- Use your ensemble to highlight different composers or communities

Engaging others

Who can help create and sustain our mission?

- Is there a way to involve the church or community at large?
- Can you create a sense of ownership with your volunteers by giving them tasks?
- If your goals seem out of reach, who can you rely on to modify those goals?

Spiritual growth

- How do we connect with God?
- Do you feel comfortable leading others in prayer? If not, is there someone you feel would perform that role well?
- Is prayer an integral part of your rehearsal? Have you tried to make it so?
- Besides prayer, what are some other ways where you can connect spiritually with your choir members?

About these areas

The first category defines our choir's *mission,* what the choir does aside from singing songs. This may mean performing services to the community like recording works for the local radio station, singing the national anthem at baseball games, and participating in the local community chorus.

The Spirit of the Choir

The *aspirations* of the choir are the most compelling reasons for people to join. Going out of the country, participating in mission work, performing large major works, or more, all fall under *aspirations*. Aspirations bring members in the door!

The third question involves *engaging others*. When people feel involved, they do more! If each person feels like he or she has a job to do, they're more likely to stick around and take on other responsibilities.

How do we move some of our volunteers from "occasionally involved" to "somewhat involved," or from "somewhat involved" to "very involved?" We give them jobs! When choir members feel important, they want to do more. It's our job to make them feel important!

Last, we look at the *spiritual* nature of choir. This can mean a general level of spirituality or a specific religious idea, if working in a church. We use our bodies as expressions of worship. Though prayer is one form of worship, some people's way to worship is to bring snacks to rehearsal or sharpen pencils, run sectional rehearsals, coach newer members, fellowship after rehearsal, or provide water are an extension of worship in our daily lives.

As choir directors, we must act foremost as spiritual and musical leaders – even if we don't necessarily feel musical or spiritual ourselves. It's been said that "if our bodies show up then our minds will follow." Non-musical acts like putting music in folders, buying pastries, or turning on the air conditioning are all acts of worship. When we are here doing the work, our spirits eventually follow.

Caring for Your Choir

Our choir's spirit gives us the excitement that focuses our rehearsal. We become engaged, prepare our spots to rehearse, enlist our group, have a few laughs, and learn along the way, all because we are motivated by our mission, our vision, and, of course, our Creator.

9.
Connecting

Why do choir members keep coming to rehearsals when they could be doing anything else? A sense of obligation, a feeling of connection, and a job to do all connect us with our choir members.

Special events – things to work for

Singing every Sunday, we probably think that the goal for us is to continue singing, week after week, as we prepare for the next Sunday, the next Christmas, Easter, and so on *ad infinitum*. In a sense, this is true. Our primary function as church choirs is to provide special music for worship.

How unexciting would life be if this was all we did!

We provide a social outlet, a connection with one another, activities outside the home, the opportunity to travel, volunteer opportunities, and a host of other events.

Caring for Your Choir

In a way, we're kind of like the USO of the church; we go anywhere, we do anything to bring people together.

If all choirs do is rehearse for Sunday mornings, then there's no excitement. It's necessary for us to do more. Here are some opportunities any of us can do:

- Host a choir retreat at an out-of-town retreat center.
- Take a trip domestically or to another country or arrange a mission trip.
- Host a guest choir, such as a traveling school/college choir.
- Fundraise for a cause, or for your own music.
- Sing at a local baseball, basketball, or football game.
- Volunteer to get tickets for a local music event.
- Sponsor some of the local high school or college singers as special members of your choir.

Retreats

Choir retreats, even local ones, can be a lot of fun! We spend several hours rehearsing, a bit of time eating, time fellowshipping, and some time for activities. The main objective is to rehearse for several hours in a concentrated format. During breaks, bring food to share and spend time eating together.

Some choirs go out of town and spend the night at a retreat center. Many denominations have retreat centers that can be rented for a low cost, and some hotels will cater to choirs, providing pianos for rehearsal spaces. In between rehearsals, choir members shop and explore the sights in a local town, spending time together in a much more concentrated way than they would if they just rehearsed on campus.

Trips and tours

Tours involve a great deal of logistical work such as negotiating with airlines and hotels, communicating with performance venues, keeping track of payment accounts, watching out for members' medical issues such as food allergies, chronic illnesses, and walking abilities, and conducting concerts in various unknown locations. Tour companies can help with a lot of these extra issues – for a price.

Despite the negatives, the level of camaraderie on a tour – especially an international tour where many in the choir don't know the local language – is unmatched. The intense amount of close time, the shared experiences of visiting historical or cultural sites, the excitement over practicing and preparing to travel, and the closeness that develops from having to live together for weeks at a time do more to cement the choir together than anything else.

Hosting a guest choir

College choirs often conduct tours in the spring semester or summertime. As someone who used to lead these college choir tours, they can be excessively expensive and exhausting for the directors. As hosts, we often give these directors a respite. The great connections provide excited audiences, wonderful meals, and beds for students to sleep in. It's one of the great joys for the touring choir and for the host choir.

In smaller towns, a college choir concert celebrates the community, where energetic voices often perform masterful literature. When I directed college choirs, students shared stories of the amazing hospitality, spoke highly of their host families, and felt close connections highlighted by the stories shared as we pulled away the morning after a concert.

These interactions often serve as a reminder that the human capacity for giving is very much alive and well.

When hosting, church choir members have similar stories, thrilled at taking in students who might be younger than their own children. They speak of the excitement and energy of the young men and women who performed just a few hours earlier. Some hosts speak of the joy of having their houses full of voices again.

Fundraising

Fundraising is perhaps the most unifying force of the choir program. We need money to hire singers, money to procure the orchestra, money for paying royalties or renting orchestral scores, money to fund the choir website, and money for advertising our fundraising and our concerts. Everyone in the choir understands the need for fundraising. Aside from concerts, it's the most visible thing we do.

It makes sense that fundraising efforts are well attended.

Connecting

It can be a wonderful treat to host several fundraisers throughout the year, many which already been described – choir contests, lunches for music camps, running sound and light as volunteer stage managers, hosting the dinner theater and silent auction, and an annual market. Each presents challenges, and each contains ways to work together as a team.

In my choir's fundraising efforts, we act as stage managers, providing space for groups to sing, setting up music stands and pianos, making sure stage lights are available, and setting the air.

My choir's workers for choir contests enjoy hearing the choirs – some as young as fourth graders. I enjoy working with the directors, seeing their choir programs grow year after year. These directors are exciting to watch as they work with their groups, often bringing large throngs of children that they seem to manage effortlessly.

Our dinner theater features many of our members. The more artistically minded singers create everything from quilts to paintings. The thrifty ones bring furniture, lamps and items that will garner a small profit, and the musically minded do what they do best – they sing. Our culinary artists prepare food – lots of food. Our dinner-theater sells out every time and we are limited only by the capacity of the room. Most of the church gets involved in the event, bringing in huge groups.

All these events give choir members activities and things to do outside of their normal day. They all know what these events are for, and are motivated to keep doing them, year after year, because the payoff is both the financial well-being of the choir and good standing in the community, offering ourselves and our spaces for the good of others.

Singing for area events

A logical outgrowth of the church choir is to sing for civic events and local engagements. In past years, I have taken the church choir to sing the national anthem at baseball games, a fun and exciting event that seems more like a tour, even though it's just one song on a ball field.

Choirs naturally can sing carols in the community, creating good relations with neighbors. Together with other ensembles, a choir can create large massed choirs for major works or interfaith events. While all these are helpful at connecting the bonds between choir members, they also give us a chance to practice our art in the community.

Other events

Projects like these and more are essential to connecting the choir to one another and serve as a reminder of our real mission – connecting with through service. There are plenty of opportunities for service – supporting local theater and community choruses by taking tickets, presenting unique programs and lectures that may have nothing to do with music, and creating mission opportunities are all ways that we can serve others.

Connecting

Writing to the choir

My most important task during the week is staying in touch with the choir. I don't preach to them; that task is best left for Sunday mornings, but I always write to them.

I began this weekly task years ago, after deciding that I needed to write more. At first, my writings included the rehearsal order on one side of a piece of paper and a short memoir about the music on the other. There might be some instance of my own personal involvement with the music. As time went on, I began receiving email responses from the members. Some people read my musings just to respond, providing another connection.

Since we travel, I wrote about travel tips. When it was time to organize I wrote about organization. When we learned different pieces, I discussed the composer at hand. As philosophy of what we're doing came into focus, my essays considered why we sing and how it will affect us.

When disruptive events like the flood happened, I sent out a quick call for help. When choir members passed away, I put out notes about the upcoming memorial services and what we would sing.

Regular writing to a friendly audience gave me confidence in my own writing ability. I spoke of improving the music and falling in love with music in my weekly writing. The more I wrote about music, the more I fell in love with writing for others, too.

Want to feel powerless? Conduct a choir. Want to feel heard and loved anyway? Write to them, too.

PART TWO:
Rehearsals

10.
Pacing Rehearsal

Introduction

7:28 PM

I walk into Room 203-204. Somehow, I've managed to keep the pencil behind my ear, even though I had just been looking for it during bell rehearsal a few minutes earlier. Debbie set the water out already, thanks to the little cart that we've somehow kept all these years. I've already set my music out, in order of appearance. The rehearsal order is written on the white board in the corner of the room, though sometimes I doubt anyone looks at that board. But then I remember, I always look at the board because half the time I can't see my paper copy.

7:29 PM

Last minute stragglers come in, folders in hand – even Bill makes his way to his chair in the Tenor section. The gang's all here, *I think to myself. People are talking about their day to one*

Pacing Rehearsal

another. I dread the last minute. I'm preparing myself for the next ninety minutes – one last inhale before the rehearsal begins.

Rehearsal is just an exhalation of energy for us. For the choir, who get to see and sing with one another, it's a joyous, funny, silly, and exciting occasion. For me, it's where I feel my whole self, working out all the musical things that seem to have popped up since last week.

7:30.

I'm already standing on the podium that Philip built for me. But I'm not thinking about that. I raise my hands in a slow, methodical motion from my sides, hands cupped with palms up, preparing a deliberate "U" as a motion for everyone to stand. The time for preparing is over. Now the warm-up, the transition from normal time to rehearsal time, has begun.

A long time ago I read a study about seventh grade band students who were asked to rate various instructors based on their perception of the conductor's approach to the podium. As a part of this experiment, some instructors were asked to walk up to the podium with shrunken shoulders. Others were asked to step up with good posture and eye contact, and still others with some variation between one and the other. Each band leader conducted one measure of four beats, and then left the podium while the students were given an evaluation of the director.

I'm reminded of that study every Wednesday when I reach the podium for the first time because, like those band conductors, my group of adults responds to the perception of my approach. As I begin the warm-up, I show the posture I want them to feel in their own bodies. I model the breath I want them to do, and I open the rehearsal with a safe space that they can feel comfortable to make music in.

Hardest pieces first

It makes sense to do this because when our minds are fresh, that's when we're most able to learn and grow, and that happens at the beginning. Plus, putting more familiar songs closer to the end acts as a "reward" for concentrating so hard on the earlier pieces of music. Above all else, don't bog down; rehearse hard sections a little at a time, and then move on to the next section.

Average adults have an attention span of about twenty minutes, so going longer on the same piece of music risks the possibility of boredom, fatigue, and/or just plain obstinacy. This brings us to our second secret of pacing:

Vary the repertoire

After working on a difficult section – note that I didn't say an entire piece, just a section – for at the most fifteen minutes, move on to another section or another piece of music. Varying the music can be enough to start the twenty-minute attention clock over again. Never spend more than fifteen minutes on any one section, even if it's awful. If it is, make the rehearsal spot smaller, and get through it, so that we come away with one successful section – even if it means just a few measures.

Now that we've limited our rehearsal scope, let's talk about the next pacing trick:

Pacing Rehearsal

Easy music first

"Ladies and Gentlemen," the director says, "I'm so excited to teach you the Haydn *Nelson* mass!" The choir murmurs excitement as they open their collective scores. He tells them to turn to the Credo, find the section marked "in gloria dei patris," a nice four voice accompanied fugue, and sets them loose in the first rehearsal.

The choir hates it in the first ten minutes.

Choirs must feel successful to want to keep coming, and if they don't feel successful, they won't come! So, it's important, especially with volunteers, to start small. Teach sections that are homophonic (hymn-like) or unison before teaching parts that are independent or fugues, where everyone sings their melodies at different times. In time, introduce the hard parts gently. Let them feel their way through it because they know easier parts are ahead. The entire work doesn't have to be prepared perfectly in one rehearsal. But when it's time to learn the hard parts, use my next pacing trick:

Sectionals

Sometimes it's just us armed with a piano. We have no accompanist, and the closest pianist is literally on the other side of the planet. If possible, when it's time to start learning these tough sections, get help. Ask the accompanist to lead one or two sections. Ask a choir member who may have some piano chops to play through her part while the rest of the section sings along. This does two things: first, it requires a change of rehearsal space, listening to another person, and allows for a different perspective from another leader, all which restart the attention span.

The bottom line is that we're always beholden to people's attention span. To have a strong rehearsal, we must keep the variations up, or we'll fall flat, making the learning process even longer.

II.
Rehearsal Patterns

Preparing the order

We prepare a rehearsal order to make the *clock* the ultimate master. It can always be blamed for successes or failures, and can be used to create an exciting, wonderful rehearsal. Though we will talk more about rehearsal techniques in a later chapter, here are a few things to keep in mind.

Ten-to-fifteen minutes

We don't rehearse any one section for more than ten or fifteen minutes. Why ten-minute increments? Research shows that adults' attention spans last only twenty minutes. Spending thirty minutes reviewing the same song, section or passage gets very tedious.

Caring for Your Choir

Divide and conquer

We use good singers, people who can play piano and singers with choral experience to help teach notes. If our good singer possesses limited piano skills, we still use them, pairing them with a pianist.

What if I have no good singers? I find someone outside the choir who teaches notes. I also make sure we still use the same technique of ten-minute increments. Alternatively, get a good singer with a loud voice who can model and demonstrate to the others how to sing their part, even if it's *a cappella*.

Manage the bites

If the work is especially long or difficult, we plan smaller sections to rehearse in the ten-minute segment. After all, there are no rules that say we must sing through entire pieces of music. If it's super difficult, rehearse one or two pages at a time, using that ten-minute focus time to its advantage.

Clock rules

Sometimes choristers love to ask questions in rehearsal. Others want to go back and re-rehearse something that didn't go well. All this slows down the rehearsal pacing. Once hitting the end of an allotted time for a piece of music, we must move on to the next song. Help your choristers understand that our timed schedule is more important than missed notes.

Rehearsal Patterns

Varying the activities

Our ten-minute segment doesn't have to include only singing through the part. Other techniques include:
- Chanting through the words
- Clapping rhythms
- Reviewing dynamics or vowels
- Using movement to create rhythmic motion
- Checking tuning

Using these patterns will create the frameworks that we'll use to create a successful rehearsal. Next, we'll incorporate them into the rehearsal plan.

12.
THE REHEARSAL PLAN

The warm-up should always start rehearsal. Though it assists vocally, its main goal is focusing our state of mind. If we're working out the problems of the day like the fire alarm being set off or the sound system not working, it's hard to stay focused on which person is singing the wrong notes. As leaders, we must shake off the mental dust and dirt that accumulates during the day.

The warm-up separates into three parts: the physical, the breath, and the voice.

Physical

The physical part of the warm-up includes preparing the torso, arms, legs, and spinal column. All these can be exercised in a limited fashion with any age group. Make sure the choir is standing, if they are able, and do this as

The Rehearsal Plan

soon as the clock strikes the rehearsal time. It signals to the choir we are beginning rehearsal, and it begins the process of focusing our attention. *Don't start with the piano.* Here are some physical warm-up examples:
1. Rolling the head
2. Rotating the shoulders
3. Stretching the arms from one side to another
4. Shaking out the hands

Breath

Warm-ups involving the breath are next. These are exercises meant to demonstrate upcoming rhythmic problems, or just activating the breath. The hands can be placed on the abdomen for additional focus of the breath. Remind the choir that their breath should come from down low – especially the high voices who must use that breath to reach the high notes. Here are some exercises for the breath:
1. Exhaling with a "ch" after a good, low breath
2. Breathing in and exhaling on "s" for a specific number of beats.
3. Using "ch," or "k," chant a rhythm that the choir repeats back to you. (You can even isolate a difficult rhythm that will appear during rehearsal.)

Vocal

Start the vocal portion of the warm-up immediately after the breath. I like to transition into it with a technique called a "yawn-sigh." This uses an "oo" that begins in the head voice and transitions downward into the chest voice.

Caring for Your Choir

It also gives me a second to decide what the next warm-up will be.

Here are some warm-ups:
- Start with the syllable "mi." Count four repeated pulses on a bottom note and then move upward by step to the third scale degree and back down. (Do, Do, Do, Do/Do-Re-Mi-Re-Do) All this should be done without piano.
- On the syllable "ooo," demonstrate a five-note descending pattern (So-Fa-Mi-Re-Do) and descend by half steps. Again, do this without a piano.
- An alternative of the above exercise is to use the syllable "Mum" with the same pattern, except going up five notes (Do, Do, Do, Do/ Do-Re-Mi-Fa-So, So, So, So/ So-Fa-Mi-Re/ Do-So-Do-So-Do.) These can be done quickly and help with range extension. Again, practice this faster and without the piano.
- Now, moving to the piano, begin the first range extension exercise, such as an arpeggiated chord Do-Mi-So-Do', Ti-Do-Re-Do-Ti-La-So-Fa-Mi-Re-Do and continue ascending by half steps. Use the syllable [ee] until the top note, where I switch them to [ah].
- Transition to the next exercise with a yawn-sigh
- Another great range extension exercise is to sing the syllables "I love to sing" using

The Rehearsal Plan

      arpeggiations, starting on the fifth note of the scale, So-Do'-So-Mi-Do.
- End with a yawn-sigh, giving a chance to move from the piano back to the podium.

This Sunday

When starting rehearsal with the piece to be performed this Sunday, it is important to go through the piece from beginning to end first. This allows you and the choir to know exactly where the problems are, and it gives both you and the ensemble a chance to feel what the entire piece sounds like. I mark the difficult spots during the first run-through by folding the corner of the page closest to the problem system of music.

After going through the work, review the places that are difficult or need work that you have marked. Then perform the entire piece again, making sure their newly solidified spot seamlessly connects to the other material.

Alternate first piece – the hardest

If, on the other hand, the music for a particular Sunday is easy, you may want to begin with the most difficult piece of music. In this case, find the hardest spot and practice that area first, followed by the next hardest spot, and the next, until you've got a good handle on the most challenging spots. If the piece is coming up soon, go through all it. Otherwise, put it away in favor of your next-most difficult piece.

Caring for Your Choir

Announcements

Announcements can drain the energy from rehearsal, so they need to be placed in a spot where they won't be as invasive. I put them right after the opening song. This way, any latecomers have made it into the rehearsal, the first song, requiring the most concentration, is complete, and there can be a break as we prepare for the second-most difficult song. Announcements can also be placed in the choir's newsletter or in the rehearsal order if they are printed out. This will keep it from interfering with your rehearsal.

Ending the Rehearsal

Now that all the music in the rehearsal order is finished, it's time to end. It's important to celebrate the end of rehearsal by creating a special ceremonial ending. This usually involves creating a circle and might involve singing. Here are some suggestions for ending rehearsals:

- Ask for "joys and concerns." This gives choir members a chance to hear from one another if there are challenges in their lives.
- Write a simple "ending chorale," use a hymn, or sing something like the Lutkin *The Lord Bless You and Keep You.*
- Read something inspirational to the choir – but only a few sentences.

Most importantly:

- Tell the choir "Thank you."

The Rehearsal Plan

Starting with a warm-up, using the twenty-minute attention span rule, preparing our most challenging music first, and creating a closing ceremony enables a successful rehearsal where our singers will want to come back week after week.

13.
Managing Rehearsal

We've picked it. We're excited by the music. Now – how do we teach it?

Introducing a piece of music

Begin at the beginning. End at the end. Repeat. Repeat. Repeat.

This is how to bore the choir to death.

Many of us have been bored to tears by sitting in rehearsal with directors who followed the "start at the beginning and repeat" approach. We diligently read through each piece from beginning to end, traverse to the next, and the next, and so on. In that final level of *sameness* that can plague choir rehearsal, eventually our volunteers drop out, deciding that they would be better off doing something else.

Managing Rehearsal

It doesn't have to be that way. We have a few ways to introduce a new piece: "here's a taste" or the "only part that matters."

The only part that matters

In the only part that matters, choose a section that has an interesting beginning, middle and ending. It may come at the start or end of the music, or it may be a calmer middle section. What's most important is that it has a noticeable ending – a fermata, a strong cadence, or a closing right before a reprise or new section. We practice only that section, ignoring the rest of the piece so that we can prepare for a mini performance during the ten- or fifteen-minute rehearsal segment. We pay attention to the notes, the rhythms, the cadences, the vowels, and other details. Most importantly, we *choose a section the choir can effectively prepare and perform in just one rehearsal.* If a section seems undoable, find a smaller, more manageable section.

Sometimes, when we choose this method of introduction, the choir surprises us by how quickly or slowly they learn the section. If it's quick, we either move on to the next piece in our rehearsal order, or increase the size of the section. If the choir isn't picking up on the music very quickly, take note during the first reading of the part they're doing well, and only focus on that section. The point is to give them an *early taste of success* as they read through the song.

Here's a taste

The other method, here's a taste, is better for easier pieces of music. If there is only one somewhat difficult section, rehearse that first. Next, go back to the beginning and sing through the whole song once without stopping. Even though they may be reticent, continue to plow through the song, giving little feedback. The main idea is to provide a general feeling of how the piece sounds. When that first read is finished, you have the option to go back to one part, or go to the next piece, depending on time.

Here's a taste can be adapted for sections of a song too. If the whole song is too difficult or too long for the choir in one setting, use this method in your *favorite* section. Chances are, if you are excited about it, your choir will be too.

Teaching the notes

Now that we've given them a taste or sung through the only part that matters, we locate the most difficult section for the second rehearsal. We isolate it into manageable parts by dividing up this new section. Are there polyphonic sections, where everyone starts at a different place? Is it followed or preceded by a homophonic (hymn-like) section? Is the contentious section filled with difficult leaps? Is there a part where the leaps are more extreme? Does the melody repeat?

We identify the problem section and start with it. First, if the choir reads well, have them try it. If not, attempt the following:

Managing Rehearsal

Sectionals

A choir member who plays the piano, your accompanist, a former/current choir director, you, or a hired assistant can all help teach notes. Choirs are about everyone; not just "us and them," so it's important, when possible, to engage others to rehearse your choir. (I have a hard time giving up my big chair too, but it's good for all of us.)

Sectionals don't have to rehearse Sopranos and Altos together and Tenors and Basses together. Two-part sectionals might be S/B and T/A, or a combination of the most problematic voice parts to put them with you. Variety is key here; don't always just choose the men in one room and ladies in another.

Two-by-two

Sometimes in full-choir rehearsals there may be a need to reinforce some notes. A great method for small problems is two-by-two, where two sections of the choir sit back while the other two rehearse. This is great when used on a limited basis. Identify which parts are having the most trouble and separate them out. If only one part is having trouble, pair that section with another, more confident section, only teaching small excerpts lasting no more than a page. If necessary, rehearse the other two sections that were left out.

Never rehearse one part at a time unless the notes are so intricate and the leaps so tricky that it needs to be looked at individually. It's more important if splitting music into two-by-two in full rehearsal to move quickly to not waste the inactive singers' time.

If a particularly hard spot comes up for one part, stop and focus on that individual part. Sing through it or have the pianist play the offending intervals. Have the group sing that small excerpt, and then put it back with the other section. If it sounds especially good after this extra attention, tell the rest of the choir what a good job that section did.

Dictated notes

If the choir seems fine when rehearsing each part alone but having difficulty when collectively rehearsing, try dictating the notes, or singing note-by-note. Each chord is sung out of tempo, and as you point, the choir moves to the next note. After successfully practicing the notes together, have the choir sing the problem section with a slow tempo. Eventually speed the excerpt up to tempo.

If all else fails…

If, after all the note banging with the accompanist, going through individual parts, and isolating different sections results in little improvement, sing with the section *a cappella.* Sing with the section on their part with no piano. In a study posted in the *International Archives of Otorhinolaryngology,* singers consistently matched human voices about 40% more accurately than the piano. By doing this, they connect with our voice. No matter how many times people hear the piano on their part, hearing it with the voice connects them to the music.

Back in context

Once finished with the section, make sure to put the spot in context by integrating it either into the section before it or immediately after. This creates a sense of accomplishment, as now the singers can see where they've come from and where they're going.

Ignoring as reward

Choir members are paradoxically shy. They are usually full of personality, loving, and lively. But too much attention on individuals or single sections never comes out well. They freeze up if they know you're watching. Sometimes our best motivation is to ignore them.

Keeping it real

As you prepare your rehearsals, try to predict which sections will need a lot of individual work, and which will go quickly. Of course, some of this requires knowledge of your own choir, but there are some indicators in the music of where you'll need to spend more time teaching notes:
- Counterpoint, such as a fugue
- Difficult leaps through a passage.
- Fast rhythms or words that might require extra attention.
- Unusual harmonies, such as jazz chords, close harmonies or music that doesn't seem to go where expected.

Caring for Your Choir

Conversely, look for sections of music called "gimmes." A "gimme" is a section or piece that the choir can read at sight. They can be songs that the choir knows well or pieces that have some of these qualities:
- Homophony
- Easy melodies that move predictably
- Unison, slow lines where you could sing along, if necessary, to teach

Place the harder materials first, using some of the techniques outlined above. Never work too many hard sections at one sitting. If you've spent a great deal of time with a difficult section, try to work on an easier section that the choir can perform well.

Pacing the rehearsal is a balance. Re-rehearsing pieces or sections that are easy will ultimately bore your choir, while practicing pieces that are difficult repeatedly will discourage and frustrate your choir.

Here's a pattern that I regularly use for rehearsals:

7:30 – Warm-up

7:40 - Sunday's anthem
    The hardest part goes first.
    Run through the entire piece.
    Review problem spots and turn in for Sunday.

7:55 – Announcements

8:00 – The hardest song that we'll do in the next month.
    Hardest part first
    Run-through entire piece

8:05 – Sectional Rehearsals: S/A with me in the other room; T/B with the accompanist in the choir room.

Managing Rehearsal

    Practice hardest section of song #1
    Practice hardest section of song #2
    Practice hardest section of song #3, which comes up soonest.

8:15 – Still in sectionals: Rehearse the rest of Song #3 (if possible)

8:20 – Return to full rehearsal: rehearse the portions of Song #3 from sectionals.

8:25 – Rehearse the part of song #2 from sectionals.

8:30 – Rehearse the part of song #1 from sectionals.

8:35 – Run-through "gimme" song or next Sunday's anthem. -

8:40 – Practice a moderately challenging upcoming song (but not too challenging)

8:50 – Rehearse a fast, rhythmically exciting song that doesn't need a lot of extra work, to leave the choir on a good note

9:00 – Ask for joys and concerns, pray, have snacks, and go home.

Closing a section

Finishing a song or song-part can be one of the most challenging times in rehearsal, as we always want it to be positive. If it's difficult, maybe recapping will be more harmful than helpful, so it's important to find a portion where the choir can feel successful, even if the recap is just a few measures of the affected section.

Caring for Your Choir

Mini performance

Sometimes we've got a great block of music that's ready. Make a performance! Have everyone who is able stand and "perform" the section without stopping. We have spent time looking at parts, correcting, stopping, and restarting, and checking to make sure everything is ready. Even if it's not perfect, it's always good to take a step back and admire the work you just finished.

Parts to whole

Another successful reward for finishing a job is the part-to-whole method. You've just finished practicing the tough section, and it's preceded by the section you already know. It's not quite long enough for a mini performance, so what do you do?

Integrate the recently polished section into the song.

Check the part immediately before or after the problem spot. Can the choir already sing it? Does the choir know it, and if not, can they read it reasonably well? If they can't, can they at least sing through the few measures preceding or following the excerpt, so that they'll feel successful?

The best way to do this is if the section being polished is closer to the end. At that point, we can work through the problem section and follow it up with the ending, allowing everyone to feel good. We've given them the sense that they've finished successfully.

Managing Rehearsal

An unsuccessful ending

Occasionally the part-playing goes poorly, the choir doesn't get it, and all hope might be lost. Before throwing in the towel, try listening for a section or a few measures that sound acceptable. Have the choir return to those measures to give them a sense of closure and remind them that they will continue working on those pieces next time. This acknowledges the fact that rehearsal is not an instant destination, it's a journey.

If you believe in your heart –most of us do – that your choir can accomplish a piece of music, they will believe it too. Dreaming, for choir directors, is infectious. When we believe that we can sing anything, we can. If we're constantly worried that our colleagues will think less of us, our teachers won't acknowledge us, and our efforts won't be worthy of the concert or the service or the congregation, we ultimately become our own worst enemy. We don't look at the pieces of music unrealistically of course, but we do try to remain positive.

Occasionally, the piece may be too much for the choir or for us. In that case, we substitute it immediately, looking for easier songs that might help teach some of the skills our choir lacks before tackling that song again.

14.
Final Rehearsal

The logistical rehearsals

At some point, each of us must lead our choirs into a concert. This is when rehearsals begin to change. A new type of rehearsal is required: the final rehearsal.

The final rehearsals before the orchestra are ideal to practice the logistical issues and fixing the occasional note or nuance. The most important things we can practice in these final rehearsals are transitions between movements or songs, getting the music in order, standing and sitting cues, how to enter the choir loft, and identifying a person to cue the choir to stand.

Where to stand and sit during the concert also needs to be worked out in advance and communicated to the choir, so they can mark it in their music. Finally, transitions need to be practiced, such as connecting between movements,

Final Rehearsal

especially if the choir has an immediate entrance at the beginning of a new movement.

Seating

During regular rehearsal, the choir usually sits wherever they wish, with no directive to their placement. With newcomers, place them next to strong singers to get them started, but after some time, allow them to sit next to whomever they choose.

As the concert gets closer, this changes.

Create a seating chart of rows that considers both the logistical and structural issues in the choir. In most concerts, the bell choir members must enter and exit the choir area at different times, so they must be placed at the ends of rows, allowing them to move in and out of the choir quickly and with minimal disruption. If I have soloists that come in and out, they, too must be placed at the ends of the rows, allowing for easy access and egress.

Next is the further divide of singers into sub-sections. (i.e. Soprano I and Soprano II) This can be tricky, as not all my singers sing the same parts all the time. Usually, if I change the seating chart, it's because of voicing.

The final criterion for seating is more subjective, once the height and voice part have been factored in. The shorter singers go in front and taller ones in the back. Once that information has been reviewed, we decide on the strong singers. Stronger singers go in two different places: either toward the middle of the row, next to singers of another section, or in the exact center of each section. Weaker singers are seated next to the strongest ones, so that everyone has a person around them that they can lean on for guidance, if necessary. Once the seating chart has been completed, the choir sits in those places during our final rehearsals. To expedite where people should sit, I use index cards to show their places, along with the seating chart placed on music stands in the front of the rehearsal room.

As we prepare for this new type of rehearsal, a few things must be ready. First, the notes and nuance must be learned. The choir needs to have a sense of confidence about their music, so we can focus on the next phase. Seating must be worked out in advance. How many rows do we need? How many seats per row? Who will sit next to whom?

Once the seating chart is finished, add it to the weekly emails and the choir newsletter so everyone knows in advance where they will be sitting.

Final run-throughs

Just as important during the logistical rehearsals are the run-throughs. These are perhaps the most exciting parts of the rehearsal. As we get close to the concert, it's important to run each piece from beginning to end, so that the choir and you can get a sense of the amount of energy needed to complete the concert. We don't nitpick notes at this point, as it defeats the focus needed for these run-throughs. The purpose is to practice the actions more than the notes.

If there continue to be note problems, address those after the run-through is done.

Final Rehearsal

Once while preparing a choir to perform with a certain state symphony, I watched the conductor, a slender, dapper man dressed in jeans and an untucked t-shirt, fold the corners of his score at certain points. Later, I noticed that he would go back to those pages where he folded the corner. It served as a mid-stream reminder that something wasn't right and needed to be fixed. I thought the idea was brilliant and have used it ever since.

If a problem is near the top of the page, fold the top corner; the bottom of the page means the bottom corner gets folded. We may not remember why we needed to come back to that point, but by having the corners folded, tells us we needed to come back to that spot. If unsure, begin a little before the folded area, ask the choir sing, and the mistake will present itself again.

Another technique along the same lines is to apply sticky notes to the score at the point where something needs to be re-addressed. This way, a physical reminder lets us know where the problems continue to exist for review.

The punch list

Another technique is the punch list. After the first logistical rehearsal, review the scores, looking at all the notes. Before the night is over, create next week's rehearsal plan, outlining excerpts that need our attention. These tend to have lots of small sections and small excerpts where, using the parts-to-whole method, we review the problem spots and re-integrate them into a larger portion.

Usually there are many of these spots, so it's important not to spend a lot of time on each one – maybe 5 minutes maximum per problem. These are fun, fast-paced rehearsals because they're so varied and they need so much concentration. Often, they go quickly because there's no time to savor each moment. Once these problem areas are completed, we can do a second complete or partial run-through. These punch list rehearsals create some of the fastest uses of rehearsal time.

The last choir rehearsals

It's extremely important to rehearse the group in longer sections as the concert looms. In these last rehearsals, we sing from beginning to end as much as possible in the allotted rehearsal time. I take sticky notes and place them on areas that need review. Immediately following these rehearsals, I take notes on the problem spots, which we called the "punch list" described in the chapter on final rehearsals. Next, I send the list out to the choir so they'll be aware. They can review the problem spots in the interim.

At the next rehearsal, we start with the long list of errors, or "punch list." One at a time, we tick them off with increasing adeptness and veracity, like hungry note-vultures ready to devour each spot. Sometimes the problems resolve themselves, and a quick check will prove that. Other times we spend more time fixing those spots.

These are my favorite rehearsals. They're fast, they're intense, and they are constantly changing. They are a culmination of all the work we have done to prepare for this

Final Rehearsal

concert, and, if done right, consist of only minor problems that can be resolved quickly.

After completing the punch list, we start another complete run-through, making sure standing and sitting cues are marked. I make the choir stand for these rehearsals, so they get used to performance conditions. The goal here is to eliminate most of the surprises so that the choir adapts to performance conditions.

Finally at the general rehearsals, we practice the last logistical problem – getting on and off the stage. Fortunately, there are people more qualified in spatial visualization than I am. In my choir, I tell them how I want them to come on stage. Then we practice, and the choir members tend to organize themselves into neat rows. It usually only takes one practice, and isn't hard, but it is always necessary and puts everyone at ease. Again, we want to take all the surprises out of the performance.

Preparing for the orchestra

Up until now, the choir is used to seeing my cues just for them. They're used to me mouthing their words. But a few weeks before the orchestra comes, I must change my tactics for them and for my own practice. Are there different cues for the orchestra? Which instrument(s) get cued, and where are they located? This is a great time to practice directional cues for the orchestra. If the choir or orchestra is large, I may start using the baton. If I intend to use one, this is the time to bring it out and begin using it with the choir, carefully cuing all the entrances to the orchestra that have been neglected because I've been focused on the choir.

Occasionally, the choir might make mistakes in their entrances during these rehearsals. It's important to remind them that they might not receive cues for some of the entrances anymore, and to rehearse those missed entrances.

Final thoughts

The rehearsal process is perhaps my favorite part of directing the choir. Following these simple steps can give your choir a positive experience.

15.
Communicating

Last night in our final rehearsal of *Ye Followers of the Lamb*, the choir came together. The choir knew how much volume to use as the piece moved along. They didn't start too fast or too loud, and when they became over-excited, I gestured to remind them of the dynamics.

I know this song well. It's an old favorite from college, and after many performances, I have specific ideas as to how I want it to sound. When should I use gestures to correct? When should I stop and talk to them? These can be some of the most treacherous issues we face.

Studies show the act of performing increases the feeling of satisfaction and even happiness. However, ask any musician in a bad rehearsal and they'll confess the opposite is true. Starting and stopping a piece of music can be so disruptive that it can harm the perception of the music.

Caring for Your Choir

In my early days of directing choirs, I always pointed out mistakes. They'd sing for a few measures, and I'd stop them. They'd re-sing the same measures still incorrectly. I'd stop them again. Or I'd make them sing the same phrase slowly.

There's *nothing wrong* with starting and stopping to correct problems. As directors, we do this all the time. The difference is today there must be a sufficient, overwhelming reason to stop.

Why should we stop?

There are three reasons for an unplanned stop: reinforcing a solution, continual errors, and catastrophic failure.

Continual errors

In *The Spirit of the Lord is Upon Me*, by Edward Elgar, the phrase "hath anointed me" happens twice; once at the beginning of the piece, and the second time at the end. The note on "-noi" of "anointed" is sung in unison both times with no changes in the other notes. The first time, it's on a D-flat; the second time a C-flat. This can be extremely confusing since they are so close, and often in a first reading both notes may come from the choir. In this case, the solution is *not* to sing one excerpt followed by the other; instead, we leave them in context and hold the note until everyone agrees on the printed note is better. If no agreement is reached, we stop, sing the note, and have the choir repeat it.

Communicating

If the choir is not stopped immediately in this case, they learn the excerpt incorrectly and will take longer to relearn it. In these cases, it's important to immediately stop and correct the error, especially if there is a risk of learning the passage wrong.

Catastrophic failure

Want to frustrate the choir? Have them keep singing after they couldn't find the first note. Watch their lips and faces. If multiple people aren't singing and some are shaking their head, then stop, review the notes, and start again. If they are on the wrong pages or singing something nowhere near what is printed on the page, stop singing. This type of failure can't be recovered and requires more attention. If the notes are not known, spend time reviewing them either using two-by-two, note by note or quickly separating into sectionals.

Reinforcing

This first reason happens if the choir is already stopped. We examine the problem, maybe talking through the solution including how to find a note, clapping, or chanting on words through a missed or tricky rhythm, or fixing a vowel or other sound production issue, including tuning. These are intentional and the choir generally knows that they will be stopping and starting through a small section. This should never happen during a complete run-through. Instead, save these smaller corrections for after a run-through or when already stopped.

Pushing through the problems

It is an art to know when to keep going and when to stop and correct. Maybe someone – or a few "someone's" missed a note or two – or three. Perhaps they got back on track. There is a point where we ask ourselves if it's necessary to stop right then, or continue to the designated stopping place, and then review the problem. Most of the time, if the choir can make it through, let them. It makes them far stronger as an ensemble if they can "push through the problem," instead of constantly going back and fixing.

Sometimes the mistakes correct themselves. In those cases, we can all rejoice! Often, the problem persists, and I can isolate the problem, fix it, and reunite it with the music before and after the problem section.

Final thoughts on when to stop

Choirs prefer singing, not listening. If we can wait to fix a problem that's minor, then we should do so. However, if the problem is so blatant that it's unrecoverable or becoming a bad habit, then we should stop. If the choir recovers quickly, fold the corner, or make a face at them, and come back to fix it. Your choir will love that you let them sing.

PART THREE:
CONCERTS

16.
Just Before the Concert

Now that we've been rehearsing for a while, fixed most of the errors, prepared our orchestral parts and procured our soloists, it's time for the final part of the rehearsal process: preparing for the concert. This starts about two weeks before the orchestral rehearsal, or, in the case of church anthems, the week of the anthem's performance.

In this last section of the rehearsal process, we are responsible for three things. First, we introduce the logistics of the concert such as a seating chart, entering the stage and standing cues. Second, we finalize phrasing nuances that haven't been addressed in the main part of rehearsal. Last, we prepare the choir for the transition away from conducting them to conducting the orchestra.

Just Before the Concert

The piano rehearsal

This is it – the piano rehearsal! By now, the choir should know their music. They should be ready with standing and sitting cues. They've practiced their entrance and exit from the stage. One thing remains paramount during this rehearsal. The choir must rehearse each piece from beginning to end without stopping. Then, it's important to go back to problem areas and review them.

Much like regular rehearsals, the final piano rehearsal has a plan to keep everyone organized. A recent one looked like this:

April 26 – General Piano Rehearsal
Mozart Requiem

7:00 - Warm-up
7:05 – Complete run-through of the Requiem, with soloists
7:50 – Notes and comments, re-dos.
8:15 – BREAK
8:30 – Line-up spots and practice coming on to stage
8:45 – Laudate Dominum, from Vespers
9:00 – additional trouble spots in Requiem, if needed
9:15 – soloists dismissed; choir: review anthem for Sunday morning

If there are guest singers on some of the music, their pieces go first. In the above rehearsal, extra personnel sang in the community chorus, so the community chorus work went first, followed by the church choir music. This way we can dismiss the extra singers. The same method holds true when planning the orchestral rehearsal.

Caring for Your Choir

The orchestral rehearsal

The most important day of the rehearsal process is the orchestra rehearsal. This is the day when all the hard work and planning pay off. But how do we successfully navigate this essential rehearsal?

For many choral concerts we may get one three-hour orchestral rehearsal. These rehearsals have to have a certain amount of break time (15 minutes for every 90 minutes of rehearsal) Unlike choirs, the entire orchestra doesn't need to stay for an entire rehearsal, and usually they will appreciate if the most instruments go first and gradually players are dismissed when they're not needed.

In our Mozart Requiem example, here's what our dress rehearsal looked like:

April 27 – Orchestra Rehearsal – Mozart Requiem
6:50 – Choir in seats, warm up on your own.
7:00 – Tuning and welcome
7:05 – Introitus – all instruments, soloists, choir
7:15 – Kyrie – all instruments, soloists, choir
7:25 – Dies Irae – all instruments, soloists, choir
7:35 – Rex Tremendae (skipping Tuba Mirum) – all instruments, soloists, choir. Double dotted rhythms (single dot soprano/alto parts m. 18 and TB in m. 19)
7:45 – Confutatis – (skipping Recordare) – all instruments, soloists, choir
7:55 – Lacrimosa - all instruments, soloists, choir
8:05 – Sanctus and Benedictus (skipping offertorium) – all instruments, soloists, choir (no timpani in Benedictus)
8:15 – Agnus Dei – all instruments, soloists, choir

Just Before the Concert

8:30 – BREAK – (there is plenty of food in the lobby)
8:45 – Communio: Lux Aeterna to end – all instruments, soloists, choir
9:00 - Offertorium: Domine Jesu Christe – strings, winds, soloists, choir – **Trumpet and Timpani dismissed**
9:10 – Hostias (right after Offertorium) – strings, winds, soloists, choir
9:20 – Laudate Dominum – strings, bassoon (no clarinet), soprano soloist, choir
9:30 – Tuba Mirum – (right after Dies Irae) – soloists, strings, winds – **choir dismissed**
9:40 – Recordare – right after Rex Traemendae – soloists, strings, winds
9:50 – END OF REHEARSAL

Starting around 9:00, instruments start getting dismissed, based on the ensemble needs. Soloist movements get scheduled last to avoid the choir sitting around.

During this rehearsal, nuances, phrasing, separations, and other aspects are almost always about the orchestra – various. Sometimes it's just running through each of the sections so that everyone can get used to one another.

Breaks

Many musicians' unions will specify breaks, so it's important to schedule a 15-minute break when the rehearsal lasts over two hours. The break happens after 90 minutes. The choir can bring food and snacks both for themselves and the members of the orchestra. This is not a requirement, but it certainly does help keep our players happy; especially those who traveled far to be a part of this concert.

We hire instrumentalists who often travel far or have other jobs. Often, we are told that they come to our rehearsals with no time for dinner, so a break with food is a welcome respite.

We also sometimes swap our last break in exchange for ending early.

Marking the music

The instrumentalist's music should be marked in advance by you or a volunteer with anything unusual like breaks, pauses and tempo changes. Also mark which type of note gets the beat, so the musicians know if we are directing quarter, half or eighth notes. If we slow down, mark if the beat will be subdivided or not. Anything to save time explaining in the rehearsal is welcome.

The measures are numbered in our score and marked. All breath markings for the choir and phrasing markings for the orchestra are also written in. We've scanned and sent all the parts to the concert master or contractor. We've considered balance and the size of the ensemble and carefully chosen how many players to hire. We've decided if instruments need to be cut based on cost and balance. We've practiced our own conducting and made sure we know all the nuances and cues to demonstrate. If there are multiple pieces instead of one long piece, they're all in order on the stand before the beginning of the orchestral rehearsal.

Just Before the Concert

The orchestral rehearsal order

As stated earlier, no one likes to sit around, so it's important to not always rehearse in concert order. The best plan for these rehearsals is to start with the pieces that use the most instruments, gradually dismissing players when they're not needed any more. For sections with soloists only, follow the dictates of the size of the ensemble needed. If strings and trumpets are needed for a solo piece, and later only the strings are needed, rehearse the solo parts with the strings and trumpets first, then later strings alone.

Keeping everyone together

With an unfamiliar ensemble, sometimes it is acceptable to give two preparatory beats. This way it is totally unambiguous as to the intended tempo. Also, except when using a large orchestra or if the chorus is large, it is acceptable to direct without a baton for more control.

Adding winds and brass

If the choir isn't large, there's a danger of adding winds and brass, as they can easily overpower the choir's volume. If that's the case, a re-write may be necessary so that an organist or pianist can cover the missing brass or wind parts. This can also help save some money when things become tight financially.

Sometimes we can write missing parts into the complete organ score or start with a piano/organ accompaniment score and mark out the sections where the organ is not needed. Though this is a little bit more work, it prevents the organ from doubling everything.

The voice versus orchestra

In those final rehearsals, especially in the dress rehearsals, it's important to check for balance. The voice is an amazing instrument. One voice alone can balance an entire cadre of instruments, but only if used correctly. To accomplish this, we must use the most important tools in our battle – rhythms, consonants and resonance.

Occasionally, the choir will forget that they are competing with the sound of the orchestra, and the choir might need to be encouraged to sing more forcefully. Request this in three ways. First, ask them to sing rhythmically, making sure they are extremely precise and accurate with the note durations. Second, ask them to make sure their heads are out of the score, reminding them to overdo the consonants.

Finally, singers must use a specific set of resonators to match the orchestra. The National Center for Voice and Speech describes the phenomenon of the singer's ability:

> *One seemingly mysterious property of the singing voice is its ability to be heard even over a very loud orchestra. At first glance, this is counter-intuitive since the orchestra is perceived by us to be so much louder than a single singer. The answer to this mystery lies in the way the sound energy of the operatic voice is*

Just Before the Concert

distributed across various frequencies. The well-trained operatic voice produces quite a bit of energy around 3000 Hz.

This phenomenon is sometimes referred to as the singer's formant and involves using different parts of the head and vocal tract to vibrate sympathetically around 3000 Hertz and again around 8000 Hertz. Trained opera singers consistently use these resonators to the point that it becomes habit, even in their spoken voice patterns.

We can teach our choir to make use of this by encouraging several actions in the jaw, mouth, and vocal tract. First, the tongue should be flat against the lower teeth. Second, the lips need to protrude, increasing the length of the vocal tract. Third, the jaw must be opened – but not for all pitches. In the higher range of the voice, the jaw can be dropped dramatically. In my choir I call this a "trumpet bell." But when the pitch is low in the range, especially in men's voices, the dropped jaw edict doesn't apply. Instead, I remind the singers to focus the sound with a narrow jaw, so that the wide, low sound waves can focus outward.

Also, Make sure a clock is in sight of everyone.

Last, take a few minutes during the break to go outside, breathe, and remember to stay in the moment. Acknowledge that it truly is the last rehearsal and is the beginning of the process of saying goodbye to these works. It's a moment to hold onto, and, like all moments, it flies away as fast as it can be appreciated.

17.
Concert Day

Concerts mean goodbye to the extra singers who add so much to our rehearsals. It means goodbye to all the preparation – printing programs, making sure there are enough tables for a reception, extra rehearsals, and singing music that we know well.

Most importantly, the concert means goodbye – maybe for decades – to a beloved major work.

In April 2017, we performed the Poulenc *Gloria* with a big choir and large orchestra. We slogged through the notes to finally emerge victorious over them. Our organ was dedicated that night, housed in what then was a ridiculous spot far away from the choir, though it turned out to be an act of providence. Having it so high saved the console from floodwaters a few months later.

Concert Day

I stood outside the back doors on a crisp spring evening as audience members filed in. I was excited, and yet sad. It had been more than twenty years since I had last performed this work, and it was my first time conducting it. I breathed in the night air, trying my hardest to stay in that moment and not let anything pass me by.

My sister took several pictures that night. One shows me standing in front of the ensemble, facing the audience. Another is of our organist, Ann, practicing in her concert black, with the orchestra setup below her on the stage floor. Another is a picture of my family – my mom and stepdad, my sister, her husband, and my husband, all standing in the middle of that maroon-clad hall. Those pictures would be some of the last taken in that hall as it was. Soon it would be gutted by muddy, putrid floodwaters.

I used to get very nervous about concerts. Now I try to stay focused, but there are always many things that get in the way like the lights, the recording, the seating, or some other silly issue that no one else thinks about. Even getting up on that grey podium with the bar, sometimes I feel so much gratitude that I get to do this for a living. I practice my audience-facing bows as best I can, and afterward, we all go into the lobby to have some food.

Starting the Day Right

It's important to begin concert day like any other day. Since my concerts are on Sundays, I direct the music in services. Also, I'm still woken around 5AM to take out and feed dogs. The morning routine remains unbroken. The morning prayer is the same.

Concert day needs to be treated as every other day. The mantra "one day at a time" still applies; nothing changes.

Final pre-concert reminders

What do we address in that final rehearsal? Will the choir still sound crisp and rhythmically accurate? Will they use the physics of their voices to their advantage?

Inevitably, this stage of the game is about *reminders.* Here are some reminders that seem to come up regularly:
- Sing rhythmically.
- Look up.
- Enunciate the consonants.
- Pulse legato notes, especially if a stringed instrument is doubling.
- Most importantly, we are proud of the choir.

A sense of rhythm

Rhythmic intensity also plays a tremendous role in balancing the choir and the orchestra. This can be defined as the choirs' sense and response to interior rhythms inside of longer notes.

Robert Shaw, master conductor and choral director, used to make singers count-sing legato passages for long stretches of time to teach this technique. By singing long notes while speaking smaller subdivisions within them, the choir felt where each note started, gave more emphasis on the beginning of each long note, and created a sense of

Concert Day

urgency of motion. This urgency carried across the orchestra with precise beginnings of notes.

It's important on concert day to walk through the day one step at a time, to not get overwhelmed. Take part in the activity in front of you, then the next, and eventually the concert will come.

18.
Lasting Moments

Recently we performed our Christmas concert to a wonderfully receptive audience. It started and ended with exciting, fun songs from movies and familiar Christmas carols. As the concert went on, I marveled at how quickly it passed. It took months to get to where we knew our notes, practiced standing and sitting, prepared to sing with an orchestra, and added all the breath marks and diction marks. Just like that, it's over.

We don't get to hold on to any of this. Music, as a temporal art, is fleeting. We sing each note in performance only once, and then it's gone. We move to the next note or next piece, leaving what we just did in the past, never to be repeated.

There's only one moment that we get to savor what's just happened – the spot between musical selections. We have two ways to do this: acknowledging the applause of

Lasting Moments

the completed piece and centering ourselves before the next piece.

Acknowledging applause

When do we bow? For how long? Do we step off the podium? After many, many concerts, here are some tricks to acknowledge and thank the audience.

Before the music

First, connecting with the audience happens through music. Nobody comes to hear long explanations, and nothing stops the excitement of the concert quite like a long discussion of a piece of music and why it's important. Get out there and direct.

When the conductor comes out, people usually clap. Acknowledge them with a slight bow. Bring the head all the way down, but the back should remain erect. Also make it a point to smile and look excited to be there. After all, the audience is excited to experience the concert.

After each piece

When a piece is over, follow a structured procedure.
- Finish the piece. Place the hands down in the same character as the music just finished.
- Step off the podium.
- Using both hands, turn toward each soloist and point to one of them. Then continue to the next soloist and continue until all the soloists have been acknowledged. If the work is newly

Caring for Your Choir

written, acknowledge the composer as though he/she is a soloist.
- Acknowledge the orchestra using a sweeping motion across.
- If the choir is your "home" ensemble, acknowledge them last, again with a sweeping gesture. (or vice-versa if the orchestra is the "home" ensemble.)
- Acknowledge the accompanist.
- Turn toward the audience, bow at the waist, looking pleasant or smiling the whole time.
- If the audience is still clapping (and why wouldn't they be?) then make a sweeping gesture to the entire ensemble, turn back to the audience, and bow again.
- One additional tip: take a moment in the weeks leading up to the concert and write down on a sticky note on the last page who to acknowledge and in what order. It certainly won't hurt to do a little work in advance to avoid hurt feelings because of a moment of forgetfulness in the concert.

Starting a new piece

Once the acknowledgements have ended, step back onto the podium. At this point, the pacing is entirely up to us. Take a moment. Savor everything. We are presenting this piece of music for the last time. Enjoy that feeling of

Lasting Moments

accomplishment because the work, at this moment, is done. All we must do now is start the ensemble.

Check in with the body. Is the back stooped over or straight? Are the shoulders relaxed? Is it clear how the next piece begins, and can that first note be envisioned? If not, take a few more seconds. Check those shoulders again. Check the back. Look at the ensemble, because by now they are eagerly awaiting the downbeat. Use the eyes – especially with volunteers – to tell them how proud you are of them.

Once the connection seems secure to the music, the ensemble, and the body, bring your hands up, and start the music.

Too many new conductors don't take a moment to pause and center themselves before starting a piece, especially if it's complicated or fast. It may take five seconds to perform a quick pause, but that time may seem like an eternity. Once it becomes second nature, centering will feel like the only way to prepare to begin a new piece.

The end

As the concert ends, use the same checklist for bows as at the end of each piece. If the closing piece doesn't use soloists, acknowledge the section leaders. Acknowledge the orchestra by having them stand, then the choir by having them stand, and finally your accompanist or any additional important people (a tour director, a second conductor, or a manager, for instance.)

Caring for Your Choir

The importance of a positive facial expression is paramount in all acknowledgements and bows. No matter how good or bad the concert went, it's important to act as though it was the best concert ever! The audience takes these cues from us, and so does your choir. If they feel like we thought the performance was good, they become more secure in their own singing and musicianship.

Leaving the stage also portrays the final mood to the audience. One inventive way involves the conductor taking the hand of the first violinist and escorting him off stage. This works well for me with my accompanist, as it acknowledges the close partnership between us.

If there are announcements or if there is a reception, this is a great time to speak to the audience. We can also end by thanking the audience for coming, and then leave the stage.

Having a plan of action and practicing that plan is vital to giving a good concert experience both to the ensemble and audience.

The important thing is this – the audience is always rooting for us. It may be jaded parents, indifferent strangers, or a room full of our closest friends, but the audience always wants us to do well.

When things start to go south, audiences always hold their breath, waiting for us to recover. Don't worry about them. We take care of our job and keep everyone together. Most likely, our audience will always appreciate us.

19.
Errors

Missed cues, nearly falling off the podium, tripping over a shoelace, having water pour in on a player from a leaky roof, missed entrances, missing music pages, starting a piece too quickly or too slowly can all happen! At the end of the day, the show goes on. We recover as best we can. All these things have happened to me in performance, and I'm not afraid to completely start over.

Early on, I worried that the performance quality was so precarious that if the slightest thing was wrong, the performance would come to a halt. After many terrible mistakes, the result is still okay.

Mistakes happen; the more important lesson is how to recover. Once I was conducting a piece where a couple and their newborn were to come out dressed as Jesus, Mary, and Joseph. The time came, and the family didn't show. At the

Caring for Your Choir

end of the song, I said to the orchestra and chorus to start at a particular rehearsal letter, and we played the part where the family was to come out *again*. I've held up rehearsal numbers with my fingers, signaling a prep beat so that the orchestra, chorus, and I could all be at the same place when everyone seemed lost. I've had people have heart attacks during concerts, fire alarms go off, and power cut out. It was all fine.

Think back to prior performances. How many items got left out? How many things went wrong like lighting cues, people entering the hall at the wrong time, power surges, or microphones that didn't come on because the batteries were dead?

What about bad cues or getting lost in the music? Though we prepared the passage correctly. something – some *glitch* happens – the choir doesn't come in or looks at you like they've never seen that music before!

It's happened to all of us. We've all made mistakes. Some are minor: getting lost for a second, turning two pages, or a loud clap of thunder. Others are noticeable but out of our control, like an instrument starting at the wrong time, a stray singer blurting out their grand entrance in the wrong measure. These happen and, in the heat of performance, there is nothing we can do.

Hector Berlioz, the great composer and conductor, encountered an error like this almost two centuries ago. While watching the premiere of his Requiem, the composer sat anticipating the grand entrance of the four brass bands. At the cue to bring in the bands, the conductor reached

Errors

down to grab a handful of snuff (apparently dipping tobacco was acceptable mid-performance) and missed the cue. Berlioz dramatically rose from his chair and began conducting the piece.

Mistakes and missed entrances do happen. If it's a problem that's out of our control, don't fret. There's not much that can be done.

However, when a musical error happens midstream, it's very important to identify a solution quickly. This is what makes for good conducting and great communication. It involves two tasks: identifying the problem and communicating the solution as quickly as possible.

Identifying the problem

Wrong notes and wrong rhythms occasionally plague us during performance. Unfortunately, they aren't the only issues. Miscounting measures, music blowing off the stand, or distractions come without warning at any time. What's a conductor to do?

Wrong notes and rhythms don't require much attention. They happen; they're over, and hopefully the singer or instrumentalist has moved on. During rehearsal we train our musicians to never dwell on a mistake. Make it proudly and move on. Sometimes our singers have an "unintentional solo." It's okay; it happens. Don't stop and glare at them; they already know.

Wrong entrances pose a much greater challenge and threat to performance. Though instrumentalists are used to counting large numbers of measures before perfectly entering on their note, pianists, singers, and bell members don't adapt to long periods of rests. Identifying a problem entrance should be easy once we know the music.

On the rare chance that music blows off the stand, musicians will generally stop playing, go pick up their music, and continue. If the music flies near you, hand it back to the player, while keeping track of the place in the score. It is far better if the choir or orchestra can get along without you for a few seconds to get the errant player back in.

Communicating the solution

Going back to our earlier example where the holy family didn't enter the second-floor balcony on time, there was no choice but to explain verbally to the choir and orchestra to play again starting at a particular letter or rehearsal number. Sometimes there's no harm in a do-over.

In another example, I started a handbell piece. After lifting my baton, someone mistook it for a start. They came in a beat early, with about half of the group coming in thinking they were late. The other half came in with me. I stopped the performance, held up the number "one" with my fingers, and began again with everyone together.

Communicate where everyone *should* be. We can mouth measure numbers, hold up fingers, or create large gestures where new sections or keys begin.

Most importantly, we must make sure that we have our ensemble's attention when something like this happens. Look up from the score. Try to make eye contact with everyone. Move the arms laterally and point to indicate something important is about to happen.

Eventually, we recover from these errors, and many times no one knows they've happened. Above all else, we keep our heads up, our chins high, and act as though it was the greatest concert ever conducted.

20.
After the Concert

In the past, we descended on a local restaurant after the concert, the choir members in their tuxedos and gowns. Quickly they ordered appetizers and confections. My husband and I posed in the parking lot for pictures in our tuxedos, adding to the elegance of the evening. Usually I arrived last, having cleaned up all the orchestral music and greeting many of our well-wishing audience members. The post-concert dinner was for *us*.

Audience members weren't allowed in our sanctum. We sat with one another, thrilled at the results of our now-completed project. Our elegant evening had finally ended. I sat next to choristers whom I got to know much better.

But behind us was a crowd left behind at our venue. We promised that someone would lock the doors after everyone went home. It was a sad state where our adoring fans – many times family members – were shut out of our reverie

After the Concert

and melee. Since I was new to this position, I didn't think anything about it.

After one concert, I cleaned up the music while many people remained in our lobby, but by the time I emerged from the stage, most of the choir had departed for the restaurant. I felt embarrassed that they weren't present anymore, but this was always the way things had been done.

As I came into the lobby after the concert, the senior pastor told me he would lock the doors if I wanted to go on to the restaurant. I felt guilty; guilty that the choir was waiting for me; guilty that someone else had to mind the mess that my ensemble had made; guilty that we were secluded from our audience members like some top-tier pop-singers worried that their adoring fans would want too many autographs or pictures.

I had an idea that would change our concerts.

After dutifully adhering to this tradition several times, I requested that the choir bring snack foods to a potluck reception. After each concert now, we go out into the lobby with our *own* reception food. Though some still went to restaurants after the performance, many stayed behind, and an amazing thing happened.

They connected with the audience.

I engaged in my usual post-concert rigmarole: stacking music, putting the stands away, and generally cleaning up. When I came out front afterward, many people were *still there!* Audience members were conversing with the choir members, and people were mingling together.

The crowd stayed for what seemed like an eternity, but, unlike the formal sit-down choir dinners, choristers and audience members mingled with whomever they wanted for as long as they wanted. When they were ready to go, they left. There was no waiting for a check to arrive; no splitting bills or having to wait on a server until 11PM on a Sunday night. The potluck reception was a tremendous success!

The reception

Why have a reception that encourages people to stay? Receptions give the choir members a reward for a job well done, but more than that, they allow audience members to connect with our best recruiting tools – other choir members. Some audience members come to hear a particular work that they might like but others come because they know they'll get a good reception with a variety of food.

Though the food changes a little, two things happened. First, the choir stayed to sample the food, and remained to clean up the hall after the concert. Second, audience members stayed behind to congratulate the choir members. In turn, our audience grew because they remain for the food made by the choirs.

Staying connected after

After each concert, there's always a letdown. The adrenaline rush has happened. The spotlights are off and

After the Concert

the hall is closed for another few months. How do we keep the momentum going?

Simple – we continue the newsletter! We advertise our next concert, creating new postcards with the concert image. We arrange a party for the choir. We send out recordings of the new work we're about to learn.

Nothing says, "get ready!" more than having a plan. The plan might become trash in a month, but just having one makes all the difference between stagnation and moving forward.

Here are some ideas to keep the choir engaged between concerts:

- Send out recordings of the new piece.
- Invite them to buy their own score.
- Create recordings of what's to come.
- Send out a narrative about the new work or send pictures of the concert venue.
- Create a video about starting rehearsal and post it on a video sharing site.
- Discuss the composer coming up in the next piece.
- Host a party for the performers midway through the hiatus.
- Send out a link to the concert so the performers can watch it at home.
- Keep the group informed about any additional information about their upcoming concert.

The important idea is to keep the group *engaged*. In the email place the next rehearsal order, when the new concert

Caring for Your Choir

will start, what day rehearsals begin, and a short vignette about music or something current. Additionally, add inspirational anecdotes or hints about something current like healthy singing tips, travel tips or even tips to keep one's pipes from freezing during the winter.

The best way to keep the choir engaged is to engage them with a newsletter!

PART FOUR:
THE INTERNAL WORK

21.
THE WHOLE SINGER

For many choir members, the choir is the main point of contact they have with other singers or the church. For some, it may also be the only social contact during the week. For this reason, it's especially important to provide more than just an excellent rehearsal.

Life cycle events

A definitive metric of an engaged choir is when members stay after rehearsal to chat. They care about one another's lives and spend time listening to and investing in one another's struggles and successes.

Keep a list of birthdays on the bulletin board in the choir room. Every month, celebrate those birthdays. Post their names in the weekly choir newsletter. Have choir members sign up to bring a cake, and stay after rehearsal to celebrate.

Occasionally, a choir member loses a spouse or other loved one. In those cases, surround that person as best as possible. Provide a caring hand, and if it isn't feasible, provide a welcoming space.

Choir members will even reach out to us in both good and bad times. When we lost our border collie, the choir members sent their love and sympathy. When we got married, the choir threw a surprise party between hand bell rehearsal and choir rehearsal. The looks on their faces were priceless, knowing they had surprised us both.

Joys and concerns

The primary mission of the church choir is to enhance the spiritual development of its members through music and singing. We take a moment at the end of every rehearsal – chancel choir, community chorus and hand bell rehearsal – to ask if anyone has joys or concerns. Often, we'll check in with one another about the status of a loved one, the success of children or grandkids, or medical updates on choir members or their loved ones.

At some churches, a choir chaplain prays at the end of the rehearsal, but we might be the one do the praying. Ask God to intervene on our behalf, helping us to find God's will and to allow us to see God's work in the ordinary.

When we are grieving, helping with sick loved ones, or hurting, it's good to remember that nothing happens without God's consent, since God created this world. It's not always a lot of comfort for those going through tough times, but maybe they can feel that love from God, or at least from us.

Joys and concerns are also a reminder that we're not just an ordinary choir; we're a choir whose primary function is spiritual. Our job is to care for one another through music, through fellowship and through function. In the church choir, our priorities are:
1. Sing Sunday mornings.
2. Sing Seasonal Concerts
3. Care for one another
4. Raise funds for other concerts.
5. Provide a social outlet.

We keep these priorities in mind as we prepare our events. What's most important? Which of our activities matches our priorities? What is less important? These five priorities allow us to decide what our calendar ought to look like.

Bringing in newcomers

Recently a new woman joined my choir but doesn't read music well. If this was a professional chorus with an audition, we wouldn't allow her in; but a religious-based volunteer church choir welcomes people with open arms.

When a newcomer appears, especially an inexperienced one, pair them with an experienced member. In my case, the newbie was placed with a retired choir director. "She's strict," I told the newcomer, "But she'll get you caught up."

The newcomer hung on to the experienced member closely, often following her as we walked into the sectional rehearsal room. But the experienced choir member changed, too. She started discussing the newcomer, reporting to me about the newcomer's progress. Her excitement at leading a newbie into choir was so evident that it has given her a level of excitement I haven't seen in a long time.

Though our goal is spiritual, we can't achieve that without connecting our members to one another. As our group grows, we just can't always make personal connections with every individual at every rehearsal. Instead, we take on the role of facilitator, connecting people together so that they can look out for each other.

Caring for our choir means knowing them, allowing them to voice their successes and worries to one another. It's not about connecting them to us; rather it's about creating a culture where they love and share their lives together with each other, and occasionally with us.

22.
LISTENING

"Joel, it's too slow..."

The confused looks on both of my choristers' faces showed the twisted, complicated feelings they held. *Do we tell him? Will it be a criticism, or will it be taken in stride?*

I was sure, given the acoustics of the hall, that the tempo was right, but when the bass player offered up that she preferred the faster tempo, I gave in.

Good choral directors know how to listen. We listen for nuance, for music, for notes and rhythms. We watch our singers to make sure they know where they're supposed to be in the score. We notice if they look lost and go back to review sections of music.

Sometimes we pray or cry with our choir members, walking with them through difficult times.

But our main job is to listen.

Listening

So, when two long-time members came forward to say "it's too slow," especially ones that had done this piece repeatedly, it was time to listen.

As directors, we don't get the luxury of directing the choir and being in the middle of it. We must rely on the experiences of our singers to gage what's happening in the trenches where the singing is happening.

It's amazing how many issues can come up when a group of people sing together. Some might stand by certain people to sing their best. Others complain about difficult members talking at the wrong time or wearing perfume. Some members might offend the others because of personality conflicts that are disguised as helpful tips.

This isn't any different from any other group of people. When people are together, there will be conflict. But we can't be in the middle of the choir all the time, so it's important for us to rely on our choir members.

When there are musical considerations, take time with them. Listen and try to adapt to their needs. Do they needing additional help in a section? Is there a particular place that needs reworking? Is the piece too fast or slow? Do they need more time to breathe?

Sometimes choir members use their positions as a power play. They find "helpful problems" and may even try to correct you. Continue with a cheerful attitude and don't allow them to run your rehearsal. As director, you always have the power to say, "We can't do that right now."

In past years, the conductor was infallible. They came into rehearsal, and no one questioned their tempos or rehearsal techniques. Even as late as twenty years ago, the conductor held a position of total authority. The advent of postmodernism has changed all this. Now, irony and individuality are celebrated. How do we adjust?

We listen. What do our members say? What are their needs? We can't meet them all, but perhaps we can acknowledge some of them. We make our singers feel important. And when we can't connect with our singers as individuals all at the same time, we can send out others – section leaders, assistants, and friends – who can connect with our singers on our behalf.

The days of "do what I say" are behind us.

A few years ago, we held rehearsal in the small chapel, displaced from our rehearsal space by a hurricane. We were singing an interesting little piece that alternated between 3/4 and 6/8 meter. Remembering my music history, I knew of several pieces that used this technique – Leonard Bernstein's *The Lark,* and Claude Le Jeune's *Revecy Venir du Printemps.* The alternating duple and triple meter – known as the Franco-Flemish style *musique mesurée* – was an important part of Le Jeune's style.

So, when I saw this in another composer I assumed – with the French name – that he was from the Franco-Flemish period. I was totally convinced of this until from the back of the room one of my choir members read on his phone how the composer had died in the mid-twentieth century.

Oops.

Listening

Since then, it became a tease that "This piece is in the Franco-Flemish style."

We're not infallible, and we do make mistakes. Our choirs – whether adults or kids – will find them and point them out, usually out of love and respect. When we listen to them, we're likely to hear the joking and the love at the same time.

23.
REJECTION

"I just can't be in your choir anymore."

"You haven't run someone off yet?"

"I can't believe you didn't put those flowers out. The former director would have always remembered!"

"I don't sing."

Rejection inhabits the director's world constantly. When we want to beat up on ourselves, we take our rejections like trophies, displaying them in cases in our minds. We can say "if only."

"If only I had talked to them differently."

"If only I had remembered to cue them."

"If only I had spent more time with them."

"If only I had made a difference to them."

"If only I had been a better conductor..."

These statements all revolve around the self; our decisions and our feelings. They don't consider that there

Rejection

are other people involved making up their own minds. It suggests self-importance, where what we do is the only reason people will stay in our choirs.

When I asked colleagues about how they handled rejection, nobody thought about rejection from choristers. Most assumed I meant romantic rejection and how they overcame it.

Rejection comes in many forms. There is professional rejection, such as being passed up for a job. Given enough jobs and enough applications, we all experience this. Most of the time we rationalize it, knowing that the job may not be a good fit or that someone closer to the hiring committee is a more viable candidate.

Personal rejection strikes much closer. It comes from family or a potential mate, where they step away for some reason. This one is hard because it can be interpreted as an immutable problem. Maybe the mate doesn't like my body type. Maybe my family and opinions don't align anymore. Maybe the friend developed new friends who understand him better. In these cases, if we care about the other person, we might wonder if it's our problem. Sometimes we substitute this type of rejection for professional rejection. We love the work, and someone wants to leave our choir; therefore, we may consider ourselves personally rejected.

Some rejections *seem* personal. People might call you names or try to bully you because they think you pick the wrong music. They might bring up your personal life or come up with random reasons to not like you. They might call your choir members or complain about you on social media.

Ignore them.

We don't have to patiently listen just because we are in a profession that demands kindness. We can choose to reflect kindness or silence. If someone in your professional circle is calling only because they need something, and yet are making fun of you or your church to others, block them.

We are not here to be everything to everyone.

The third type of rejection, the kind we experience most often as directors, is both personal and professional. In this type, the person may reject an invitation to become part of the choir because of a busy schedule or a sick relative, but we interpret it as personal.

Asking someone to join the choir carries risk. Though it's not as personal as asking someone out on a date, it's still somewhat anxiety-inducing. Overcoming this anxiety with potential choristers is like overcoming the anxiety to perform on stage. It comes with practice. It requires self-assessment.

Taking inventory

If a long-time chorister quits because the ensemble is too difficult, we may need to take inventory. "Am I pushing the choir too hard?" one might ask. "Are my rehearsals too intense?"

If we've performed the necessary inventory before this rejection happened, I already know the answer. Maybe the person can't handle the physical demands of the choir

Rejection

anymore like holding music or deep breathing. Maybe the person just lost a loved one and is still grieving. If we haven't taken an inventory, it might seem like a personal attack. We might assume we are terrible.

See how it turned into something about us?

How do we take this inventory, and what do we do with it? Writing answers down is the best way to understand and work through the inventory. First, start by asking some questions of yourself. These should help get started, but you can add your own.

- How does the choir respond in rehearsal? Do they seem happy to be there?
- Are my rehearsals organized? Do people know what to expect?
- Are my gestures clear? Is the choir doing what I want them to do?
- Have I conducted myself in a pleasant, professional manner?
- Do I show or explain passion towards the music, or am I acting in a tyrannical manner?
- Where are my insecurities in rehearsal?
- Where are my insecurities with myself?
- How are my relationships with the choir members? Do they trust me?
- Am I placing the music and its interpretation above everything else?

The answers to these questions might not always be flattering, and the answers may change over time.

Caring for Your Choir

Some questions address habits we need to form as directors. These take discipline, but are genuinely easy to assess and fix, if need be.

Others take time, like tolerance and patience. In time, we learn how to temper passion into effective solutions. We learn how to communicate better, using concrete descriptions for what we want: higher, lower, faster, slower, longer, or shorter, and we learn to demonstrate the vocal techniques needed to accomplish these goals.

The remaining issues that influence us dealing with rejection are our insecurities. At this point, we may need to do some writing. What are our biggest fears? Where do we feel like we're going to fail the choir? Where do we stop and say awful things to ourselves like "the choir deserves better than me." Where do we blame others when we're really at fault? What are we most worried about in performance, and which parts of that worry stem from the idea that someone will laugh at us?

Write out the answers to these questions in the paragraph above. Then find a friend or colleague you can trust with your confidence. Explain to them that to grow as a musician, you must start to give up some of these fears. If a friend or colleague isn't available, use a spiritual adviser or clergy member; preferably one that isn't your boss.

Take out your written notes about these fears and share it with your friend. Your friend's job is to listen without judgement; nothing more. Their job is not to offer advice or forgiveness.

Rejection

Once you have finished this process, you will have looked at your fears with another person. When a choir member comes to you with rejection, you will know if you are at fault or if you are blameless for their departure.

Most of the time, after reviewing my own fears, it's easy to find that people quit for a variety of reasons – almost none of which had to do with us. It still hurts, but it doesn't hurt as much knowing that we did everything we could, but it just wasn't a good fit.

These days I don't randomly ask others to join the choir. They just come, usually at the invitation of current choir members. My best advocates are members of the choir.

When a potential member reaches out, usually it's through another choir member. Suggest to the new person to come and sing, rather than sit and observe. The most successful recruits are people who know others in the choir.

Some choristers think that the choir is too difficult and their musical skill isn't strong enough. In some cases, despite reassurances, they drop out. This is the curse of having a good choir.

As directors, we can get rejected, too. We can be passed over for a better directing job or a prestigious musical opportunity. We can feel rejected when a lull in recruitment happens. Our bosses can fail to recognize us over and over, despite our best efforts and our finest work.

This happened while I was teaching. I managed to secure my college choir the opportunity to sing with a professional orchestra nearby. It was a tremendous opportunity that I couldn't believe had come thanks to a few phone calls and a recording. A few weeks later, the academic dean sent Christmas cards out, meticulously signing each one.

"Thank you for your work in assessment," it said.

I had done a great deal of work on the assessment committee that year, yet not a word was said about the choir. *Ouch*.

Dealing with rejection

Studies from *Psychology Today* suggest taking time to deal with the grief of rejection. We're supposed to accept what happened. We're supposed to be kind to ourselves. We're supposed to grow from the experience.

After many professional rejections, something changes in our outlook. We quit worrying about it. We quit fearing rejection or people's opinions. We step up to other opportunities. We exclaim, "Yes," when asked to lead workshops or chair meetings. We take on challenges far outside of our musical comfort zone. In short, we quit caring about what others might think.

At my church, when our performance hall finally reopened, I needed to find volunteers to run the lights and sound, so I started asking. In that time, several people rejected my requests, but I knew those rejections weren't personal. It didn't faze me at all. My internal discovery work provided enough emotional shielding from the many rejections I received. In essence, it wasn't all about me. In time, people agreed to run lights and sound on a rotating schedule every weekend.

Rejection

Betrayal

Sadly, we sometimes contend with the worst kind of rejection – betrayal. Perhaps a chorister or someone we know talks badly about us, including saying things that just aren't true. Maybe a singer moves to a different choir and tells friends it was because of us. Worse, sometimes people we know decide that our presence as the director is no longer wanted or needed. What do we do?

First, we take a quick look at our own behavior. Were we at fault? Did we choose music that was too difficult or say something offensive? If they are speaking ill of us, is it true?

Whatever the case, if it's bothering us that someone doesn't like us, then we need to pray for that other person. We pray for two weeks and can even say, "I don't like that person." It's ok; these are our own feelings. We pray for their health, and that they receive all the same benefits we received.

As the two weeks pass, we begin to develop compassion for that person. We learn that maybe they have something else bothering them. Maybe an event has triggered in their mind that has nothing to do with us. We don't take other people's problems on; after all, they don't belong to us!

If we're being offensive, we can remedy that situation easily. We ask forgiveness from the other person, or, if they left our ensemble, we forgive ourselves.

Caring for Your Choir

Don't take it personally

Rejection isn't usually about us. We may be the best director on the planet (and I'm sure you are!!) We may have the finest, most exciting rehearsal technique. Our piano skills may be legendary and only second to our vocal abilities, but if the new chorister's work schedule changed, we're going to get a "no." That's life.

If we take rejections personally, we prepare ourselves for a career full of resentment and frustration. Who wants to sing for someone who feels angry all the time? Who wants to sing for someone who doesn't love themselves too? None of us became choir directors by mistake. We remember the work that we do and its reward. We remember that we *get to* make music; that we *get to* lead rehearsals; that we *get to* inspire others and lead them into greater artistic fulfillment. Above all, we don't worry about rejections.

24.
Self-Care

3:30 PM. At the hotel. I've been up for about 12 hours.

After a late night getting home from rehearsal, I made a mad dash for the airport. I flew across Texas and ran to the convention center so I could start my shift at 11AM as a volunteer.

It's been a short night, and I'm quickly trying to raise my blood sugar, which has fallen again – and it was entirely my fault. I said goodbye to my dogs and husband at a very early hour to come here to meet some of the wonderful volunteers at this convention and to write.

I've seen several people I know – some I've known for many years. Some are colleagues, and our conversations might begin like this:

"So... How are you?"

This elicits several responses:

"Oh, great!" some will say.

"Busy," respond others.

Caring for Your Choir

And my favorite response... "Stressed."

We get it; many music teachers have already left teaching. We've transitioned into working with adults or directing in churches or have quit working in music altogether. At the music teacher's convention it's particularly glaring to see the lack of veteran teachers in their late forties and early fifties. We, who came in with excitement and yearning to give the next generation the same wonderful experience we had, were crushed by ambitious older teachers, by parents who questioned our worth, or by the very kids whose minds we hoped to fill with exciting melodies and the joy of singing with one another.

Non-musician bosses can think our jobs are frivolous; that we just exist as entertainment while something more important is coming. We may get paid a pittance to do many hours of musical work or worse, tasks that have nothing to do with our jobs and yet must be done.

Then there's the high of it all. Seeing the choir again after a week; achieving a good ending to that difficult section we've practiced for weeks. These are the moments we live for.

Our non-musical friends don't understand what keeps us coming back to the ridicule, insults, and assumptions. They've never reached the mountaintop high that comes with great work well done. They just see that we're working seventy hours a week; that we have bills, muscle pains and teach private lessons on the side.

Self-Care

One old friend I ran into recently said we take care of our ensembles so much that we rarely take care of ourselves.

We are directors who are often overworked and tired, who see each other once a year at a music convention to generically ask "how's it going;" who one day learn that our health has failed us or our friends have died. How do we care for ourselves?

Every so often, we must step away from the rehearsal process so that we can adjust our perspective to creating a better rehearsal. The stories, the experiences, the humor, and the fun experienced in rehearsal come from events both in and out of the rehearsal room, and if we don't spend time doing both, we'll never learn to enjoy our time in rehearsal.

Attending workshops about things other than music, driving or flying somewhere new for exploration, creating works of art, composing, and even building things prepares us for more robust, exciting rehearsals. There is no better time spent preparing for rehearsal than time away.

What will we find when we return? The spirit of the choir beckons us back home. It keeps us checking our email and thinking about our next project, next concert, and next idea.

Guides for self-care

In what ways do we take care of ourselves and detach from the church to focus on our own spiritual healing?

- Are we participating in non-church activities: hobbies, yard work, and other creative tasks?

- Are we making time to visit spaces either of a natural or spiritual type: beaches, national parks, or wooded areas?
- How do we cultivate our spiritual and emotional development?
- Do we attend spiritual or religious groups outside of the church?
- Are we involved in the community at large away from the choir?
- Do we look forward to spending time at home, either with a partner, a pet, plants, creative work, or household projects?

Practice gratitude

Sometimes things really *are bad*, but not often! Usually, things are just *okay*, or even *good!* Instead, our minds focus on the items we want to fix. We must look for good things, however small, to be grateful for. One person writes, "it can be the lady who smiled, the room which is not too cold, the person who was kind on the other end of the phone, or a friend who texted at precisely the right time."

Taking breaks

A few minutes, a few hours, or a few days don't matter. When we walk away from a stressful scenario, we get a chance to examine it from a different perspective. This can be as simple as walking across the room, calling a friend or loved one, sending a text, or reading an article.

Self-Care

Even though I talk about it, recommend it, and tell you to do it, I fail at this myself. I don't eat well; I do not exercise or meditate; I don't get enough rest. And when I fail, I try to forgive myself for doing so. I can always start over tomorrow to live a healthy life if I didn't do it today.

Prioritize

So many people can reach us at all hours of the day and night it makes it almost impossible to stay in the moment. Is this phone call important? Is it something I need to hear? Is this something I need to say? If it isn't, I can ignore the call or email. Can I pause before hitting send? Can it wait until later? Some of us like to have our phone calls finished before we leave, but if it means leaving later and later, we should rethink our strategy.

Change the perspective

We choir directors can sometimes get dressed down by parents, administrators, fellow teachers, and even colleagues. Will we even remember why in a week? Will we still be in this same situation in a few days? When we change our perspective, these momentary storms seem less threatening.

Pray

There could easily have been suggestions to take time off, treat oneself to tasty food, enjoy a fun experience, or create a travel escape, but not everyone likes those things. However, everyone needs mindfulness and connection, and the best way to do that is to take the time to do it. Meditation takes only a few moments and prayer even less.

Our time

We all work sixteen-hour days sometimes. We all eat too little or too much. We don't rest as much as we want, and we know it. We have families that pull at our heartstrings, students or choristers who need extra help, and concerts that are just around the corner.

There are times when it's important to stop; to skip that extra class session, to find a way to have a meaningful conversation, or to rest.

In my book *Singing in the Moment*, I discuss some of the ways we can all practice self-care. We can create more items, spend time with our friends, visit nature, take time with plants or in our yards, or practice a myriad of other things to take care of ourselves.

Nobody's perfect

We all have problems caring for ourselves when we're in a career where we're supposed to care for others. The important thing is to *try*. We try to act a little healthier. We try to treat ourselves well. We try to speak gently about ourselves. We try not to listen to others' negative comments on social media, or from casual references as they walk out of our services or concerts. We try to ignore people that demand our attention about culture war edicts or our song choices, our private lives, or our hobbies. We shut them out

Self-Care

as best as we can and plod along, trying to be unaware, hiding our sensitivities.

We seek out friends with whom we can laugh at the difficult times. Sometimes that's a spouse or a colleague who understands or at least sympathizes. We can laugh a lot, knowing they understand. And we can threaten to reveal it all in a stand-up comedy special or a tell-all, best-selling book about life in the public school or in the church choir or the cut-throat world of academia.

Over the past five years, I rediscovered my love for writing. For years, I avoided it. But when I started writing for fun – after being struck with an intense urge to write some of my conducting ideas– I realized I enjoyed it.

I travel out of town alone now to write. I also recharge my batteries, but mostly I write. I rent a space, bring lots of coffee, and get to work, creating books to help others. When I'm in the midst of something at church – a flood, a pandemic, a rebuild, or, in today's case, a major electrical problem, I think back to the week I spent in Marfa writing, or the week I spent in Wimberley in the snow, or the week I spent in Galveston with a friend, or the wonderful weekend in Smithville on a pond, spending time in the grueling Texas heat trying to formulate another chapter.

I look back at those wonderful experiences as I write the next chapter of whatever I'm working on, and I think of how *lucky* I am that I get to do this. I'm able to put my real life as a choir director on hold for a bit and live my secret identity of being a writer and photographer.

And it's intentional.

Visiting places is extraordinary. In addition to writing, my camera comes out and all I can think of is the next shot, how the moment will be immortalized and how it'll go with a later edition of *Choir Notes*. But the real thrill is when I spend time writing; engaging in another creative outlet with tangible results that I'll take home with me after two or three or even five days. During that time nothing else matters except sentence structure, content, and staying away from "be" verbs. The evenings are meant for going to eat, cooking, or watching guilty pleasures on TV.

In short, I have a hobby. I have several, in fact; working in my yard, fixing stuff around the house, and even occasionally building things keeps me occupied and out of my head. And in that way, I can be creative and good to myself.

You can too.

25.
Reconnection

And he shall be as the light of the morning...."

Randall Thompson's *Last Words of David* uses innovative, profound text that stands subservient to the magical chord progression. E minor leads to D major, to E major and finally F-sharp major. Even with a thorough analysis, it doesn't prepare us for the sublime word painting.

We learn the notes and rhythms, even though they're not easily explained tonally. We learn melodic contours and how to sing each part, but we aren't prepared to explain the blossoming of that tremendous line.

Where is God in all these rehearsals? In all this advanced work? In all our planning? When our choir sings work like this, the Presence is easy to find.

Where is God in rehearsal? Is God in the breath? Is the Divine in the vibrations? Is the Spirit in the harmonies, the dramatic shifts, or the resonance?

Yes, and so much more.

When we feel melody combined with the right texts, it is indescribable; whether it be an *Agnus Dei,* a line from Isaiah, or a Chopin nocturne, that thing happens where we understand. We want to be a part of that creation. Politics and climate change, wars, divorce, loneliness, and all the other parts of the world melt away; nothing else matters. We become one. When we perform a piece of music, we're compelled to find more music to do.

In a study released in 2013 in *Evolutionary Psychology,* an Oxford researcher found that performing musicians have a much higher level of endorphins, the substances in the brain that make us feel good. The reward for good rehearsal is performance, and getting to perform a piece of music all the way through creates the connection, releases the endorphins, and connects us with God.

The two ways we experience the divine in rehearsal are the breath and the connection.

The breath

Breath is the ultimate task of centering ourselves with the divine God. When we breathe in, we unwittingly connect ourselves with other people drawing in breath. So, if we all do it together, we literally absorb energy from the exact same source at the same time.

Reconnection

As directors, we then ask our choirs to focus on our breathing; the very act that binds us together. We ask the choir to breathe deeply and low, so that we'll have enough energy and air support to make it through a phrase. And before we sing a single note, we focus on our breath, our shared concentration with one another, our connection with the world around us and the divine.

Concentration on the breath also quiets the mind's capacity for judgement. It allows us to remain in the moment, so that we can prepare for the mental gymnastics of singing correctly.

In short, the breath allows us to simply "be still."

The Connection

As musicians, we sit on a tightrope between being swept away at the beauty, energy, angst, or raw emotion of the music, and by the technique and concentration we need to maintain to get through the music. Yes, we are allowed to feel, but not too much.

When we sing through a passage, we are moved by the technical prowess needed to get through it and by the music itself. Going back to Randall Thompson, as we're singing it how could we fail to be moved by both the music and the text?

As performers, we must rest on the razor's edge between emotionalism and functionality in performance. We can't wallow in self-pity or rampant emotionalism, or we'll destroy our chance to convey the musical message to the audience.

Caring for Your Choir

Finding both breath and connection

Yet another *Messiah* concert loomed; but this one was different.

In 2017, as I talked about in Chapter 16, we had just completed the all-Poulenc program, featuring the organ concerto and the *Gloria.* After the hall was shut down thanks to the wall of water inside, it sat as an empty, darkened shell.

Over the next four years, we waited. We waited for the other buildings on the campus to be rebuilt. We waited for FEMA grants. We waited for fundraisers. We began storing things in the hall from other construction sites.

Finally, work began. We watched as sections were torn out and restored. We waited while sheetrock, railings, air handlers, and more were added. We sat amazed as flood doors were created and installed. We picked chair colors and wood colors with designers. We discussed paint swatches and more restrooms. We picked out seat shapes and updated chandeliers.

Four years later it was the night of our *Messiah* performance. I stood in the hallway – now lit up, where for years it was empty, unable to be lit up or cooled. I couldn't believe my eyes.

There were people inside – and they kept coming. To my astonishment, people rushed into a place where I was used to being alone.

At the end, while people applauded, I looked out into our superlatively appreciative audience with a different feeling. I looked at the carpet that we had picked out together, the chairs that we had carefully matched with the wooden end caps, the lights in the rafters accessible only by an orange spider lift that seemed to belong on the set of *Aliens*.

There they were – reminders everywhere of the work that had been done. There was evidence of countless hours coming in early to make sure emergency lighting was in. Hours of matching wood stains on the doors, checking that all the keys and locks matched the correct key, taking photos of the progress, and culminating with this concert – our first in the finished space.

As I stood there on the stage, I'm sure I wasn't the only one who recognized the significance of the completed project. Maybe some audience members were only there to see the inside. Maybe some were there just to criticize and judge our performance. Looking out at that audience, I was still amazed that there were actual people in the chairs. The slow, agonizing progression from flood to project to performance seems, even now, insurmountable. Yet here we were.

I could only come up with one explanation for this – somehow a God that I couldn't fathom had made this happen.

The film director Woody Allen says that eighty percent of success is just showing up. There were so many people involved in this project – design committees and bidding committees and people who spent hours accounting where every FEMA dime went. There were advisors and advisees, meetings, and confrontations. There were furniture decisions and interior designers, contractors and architects, plumbers, and electricians and some of the most talented sheetrock hangers I have ever seen. Together, they worked day after day in the heat, in the freezing cold, sometimes even late at night, to prepare for this moment. Suddenly it was here, and I couldn't explain how it could've happened. The best I could figure was that someone else must've made all this happen.

When extraordinary events occur, it's important for us to step back and recognize that we are looking at the handiwork of the Divine. When things come together without explanation, unfathomable heights are reached, or impossible dreams are achieved, there can only be one explanation.

It's the work of the Divine Creator.

Of course, any number of synchronistic explanations can be made. I could say that the reason everything worked well was because someone in the church had project managing experience. Someone else had the background and knowledge to supervise the project because he had experience and expertise in general contracting and understood the sequence of installing items in a building. We could cite certain people who were able to get us grants to supplement our flood insurance.

The fact that these people seemed to appear at just the right time is harder to explain. Why did the project manager appear when she did? Why was the contractor just down the street at the other church before putting a bid on this one? How did the federal government, notoriously complicated in anything and everything, suddenly bring a ray of financial sunshine to our otherwise hopeless rebuild?

Standing there in that full concert hall, the answer came – this was the work of a much greater presence.

Can God be in there, too?

It's been seven years since I last performed the *Requiem* by Maurice Duruflé. I almost didn't do it, as it was the last piece I had ever conducted before leaving teaching behind.

Back then, my former community chorus didn't quite fit in the space. The choir lined both sides of the very Anglican choir loft, dutifully split in half. More choir members stood in the front. Folding chairs were everywhere, but they didn't fit, really. To see all these singers, I added a box. And another. And another. It was an OSHA violation or major injury waiting to happen, but finally I teetered on enough wooden boxes to see the organist over the dozens of singers.

As deftly as I could, I lifted the baton and began to conduct the dress rehearsal. *Stoic*: I thought to myself. Don't think about it. Linda knew something was wrong; I could see the look of concern on her face as I moved through each of the sections. It was Linda's birthday.

As we began the rehearsal of one of my favorite works with people I've known for more than a decade, my heart was heavy.

In the grocery store across the highway, I was looking for a birthday card for Linda. I cursed myself for waiting until the very last minute; I'd have to sneak that card around the choir to have everyone sign.

Caring for Your Choir

The phone rang. The caller ID said it was my best friend, Nancy, one of the few people I remained in touch with from my days in Arkansas.

"What are you doing?" I said, in our silly, sing-song voice that we used to greet one another over the telephone. It had been only a day or so since I heard from her.

Except it wasn't Nancy. It was her son-in-law.

Nancy was dead.

I held the birthday card in one hand and the phone in the other, as I waited in the cash register line. I was stunned.

"OK," is all I could get out. I spoke a few more minutes to the son-in-law and ended the call.

Setting up the folding metal chairs, I told no one. I couldn't; I'd lose all decorum and would start to cry. I did what I was supposed to do. I prepared the space, made sure my score and last-minute markings were ready. I asked God to grant me some strength to do what needed to be done that day.

I have a little trick when there are too many people around, and I don't feel comfortable right before a performance. I go outside. As people began arriving for the 6:30 dress rehearsal, I stayed outside. I sat in silence.

The lines were especially poignant that night. Old memories of seeing the opening bass part sewn in a quilt, feeling the angst of the "Hostias" all combined to create what might have been a powerful emotional experience, except I didn't need to tap into any emotions right then.

It's a funny thing how grief works. By the time we arrived at the "Sanctus" I felt sure enough to get through

Reconnection

the piece. The organist noticed I was quieter than normal, and I was in no way better, but I would be okay. The music itself pushed me forward.

Our profession as choir directors can be somewhat lonely. We spend our time working with others, allowing our own needs to sometimes take a back seat to the larger needs of the entire ensemble. Some of us might rarely admit to things going on in our own lives because we're focused outward, and because it might distract us from rehearsal. That night – the night that Nancy died – was one of those times. The loud, exuberant *in eccelsis* that blasts out from every part of the ensemble required too much power to allow for sadness.

We can't feel our own self-pity or emptiness at death when faced with great music. And in that way, music – which comes from God – is the ultimate healer. When I walked into that rehearsal room, I didn't know if I'd be able to function. Yet, when we all walked out of there two and a half hours later, I was uplifted. The music, my job, and the experience had all helped me stay grounded and out of myself.

It's in these moments that God becomes more than a vague idea. Once again, a confluence of random events had occurred. My friend's death happened in the final preparation of a powerful work celebrating the dead. A coincidence? Not hardly.

EPILOGUE

It's Christmas time, again.

Well, not really – it's the end of April, and I'm just two weeks away from the spring concert – the Duruflé *Requiem.*

I've spent the last few days prepping the scores; marking mine with the meter changes that I'll need to conduct and marking the string parts so they'll know what to play. I love pulling out the scores and studying them. For one thing, it gives me a sense of legitimacy, knowing I will be performing this piece with this score soon. I can study my scores from anywhere – much like writing. Spending time in silence, I hear the melodies in my head, imagine what the gestures will be, and revel in the idea that every decision has led me to this point; that this piece chose me as much as I chose it.

We ran it all the way through the other night, and though there are parts that need some work, it's not in bad

Epilogue

shape. But the choir needs to know – what are we doing next?

It's important to have an idea where we're going.

Once again, the piece of paper is staring at me - "Ideas for Christmas Concert." This year, a lot has happened. We're taking little trips to different parts of Texas. The desire to write a new piece of hand bell music came to me this morning in the Lowes parking lot. As always, things keep moving forward.

When I started directing, I was a young idealist with a dream who was stubborn enough to stick to it. Time progressed, as it does for all us, and I became a little more established. One day I woke up and realized I belong in this place, and it's hard to imagine life any differently.

The most important thing about caring for your choir is this: longevity reaps its own rewards. We cease being the "new director." We stop "trying new things" and become established. It takes time but is so worth it.

So, we gently walk through that first year, or he first five years of establishing routines somewhere new. We don't give up. Soon we'll be part of the establishment. Others will look to us for stability and rational thought (hopefully). In time, colleagues won't even remember a time when we weren't there. We become part of the "old guard."

Preparing for the next hurdle

That piece of paper with "Christmas Concert" stares back at me again. *Ugh,* I think. How will I ever top this year's great concerts? A preacher I know, when asked how he'll top Easter Sunday to make it more spectacular, says, "I'm going to light myself on fire."

It's tempting to go over the top, but then what?

One day, we'll have an answer, but for now it's one day at a time. Each day we choose some music and go through it. We give it an "up" or "down" vote. We choose as best we can. We look at our budgets. We bid the year and our music a fond farewell, and we start new. Sometimes we ask others for help in deciding. Often, we're forced to do this alone.

We're never alone, though. We have members in our choir who are trusted friends. We have clergy who are busy shaping their own holidays. We have other choir director friends who are doing the same thing. And finally, we have a power greater than ourselves, who knows that eventually everything will turn out right. Whatever our resource, we use it well and use it often, for we must return to the same creative well every year with fresh new eyes.

As we prepare for another Christmas Concert, another Broadway show, another great work, and another set of music, remember that we are never alone. We all are members of the Chorus of the Great Director, and though we have our part, the quality of the performance isn't up to us. It never was.

Just care for your choir.

About the Author

Dr. Joel Plaag is the choir director at Cypress Creek Christian Church in Spring, Texas. He conducts the Cypress Creek Community Chorale, two handbell choirs, a children's choir, and the Chancel Choir. After rediscovering a love of writing, he authored *I'm a Choir Director: Directing the rowdiest volunteer choir and loving every minute of it* and *Singing in the Moment: A choir director's notes on life, learning and contentment*.

Dr. Plaag was choral director at multiple colleges in Texas and Arkansas while researching and publishing on conducting pedagogy. When in school or teaching, he held positions as music director at First Christian Church of Grand Prairie, Texas; Holy Cross Lutheran Church of Houston, Texas; First Methodist Church of Brenham, Texas; quartet soloist at Temple Emanu-El of Livingston, New Jersey; and Emanu-El of Fort Worth, Texas. He founded the Batesville Choral Society and restarted the Brenham Chorale after a multi-decade hiatus. These days he also serves as cantor and pianist at Temple Israel in Schulenberg, Texas.

His major conducting professors include Professor Ronald Shirey, Dr. Joseph Flummerfelt, and Dr. Charles Hausmann. He continued his conducting studies in Romania with Maestro Ovidiu Bãlan, Maestro Robert Gutter and the Filarmonica "Mihail Jora" of Bacãu. Additionally, he studied organ with Dr. Linda Patterson and voice with Dr. Vincent Russo and Judith Gans.

Dr. Plaag holds degrees from Texas Christian University, Westminster Choir College, and the University of Houston, where his dissertation was on using Laban Movement Theory in teaching conducting. He currently lives in Spring with husband Michael and three dogs: Teddy, Freckles and Simon. On many weekends you can find him working in his yard, fixing something in the garage, or writing.

www.ingramcontent.com/pod-product-compliance
Lightning Source LLC
Chambersburg PA
CBHW031113080526
44587CB00011B/958